FIELD MARSHAL MONTGOMERY'S TACTICAL HEADQUARTERS
FROM ALAMEIN OCT. '42 TO THE BALTIC MAY '45

BURG

rg

an Surrender Signed 4 May 1945

Elbe

●BERLIN

NY

●LEIPZIG

WARSAW●

BRESLAU●

PRAGUE●

CRACOW●

T

H●

VIENNA

BUDAPEST●

BELGRADE●

ORENCE

SOFIA●

MONTY

THE MAN BEHIND THE LEGEND
NIGEL HAMILTON

Lennard Publishing
1 9 8 7

Lennard Publishing
a division of Lennard Books Ltd
The Old School, Brewhouse Hill
Wheathampstead, Herts AL4 8AN

British Library Cataloguing in Publication Data

Hamilton, Nigel, 1944–
Monty: the man behind the legend.
1. Montgomery of Alamein. Bernard Law
Montgomery, Viscount 2. Great Britain Army –
Biography 3. Marshals – Great Britain –
Biography 4. World War, 1939–1945 – Campaigns
1. Title
355.3'31'0924   DA69.3.M56

ISBN 1-85291-006-2

First published 1987
Designed by Pocknell & Co
Printed and bound in England by
Butler & Tanner Ltd,
Frome and London

Contents

A Clash of Wills

The greatest British army commander since Wellington, the most popular British battle hero since Nelson? Or a vain braggart who wore, in the words of one critic, a mantle of borrowed glory, a difficult, pugnacious prima donna whose lack of tact upset his American counterparts, and who used First World War methods to win his Second World War victories?

Opinions vary widely. Certainly Field-Marshal Montgomery – 'Monty' to his men and to the world – was one of the most controversial soldiers of the 20th century.

Born a century ago, on 17 November 1887 in a South London vicarage, Bernard Montgomery was not an easy child. His father, a parish priest, was soon promoted to Bishop of Tasmania, and from the age of one Monty's formative years were spent in Australia. Monty's father, an evangelical Anglican missionary, was away for long periods. While he urged repentance on sinners and converted Aborigines, his young wife looked after the family in Hobart, beneath the Hartz Mountains.

Maud Montgomery was no ordinary Victorian housewife. The daughter of a great Victorian headmaster, writer and preacher, Frederick Farrar, she'd been engaged at 14, married at 16. As her family grew in size – she bore nine children in all – Maud came increasingly to rule by autocratic, somewhat ruthless methods. Her will became sovereign in the Hobart household, even overruling that of the Bishop, who became more and more a 'passenger' in the running of the family.

Monty, the wild and rebellious third son, soon became the black sheep of the family, always in trouble and resentful of higher authority. When he was caught smoking his father asked him to kneel before the altar in the Bishop's private chapel and to ask the Lord's forgiveness. Father and son knelt there in prayer. At length the Bishop got to his feet, saying "Sin no more, my son – the Lord has

Monty's parents, in St Mark's Vicarage, Kennington with their first child.
Monty's father, Henry Montgomery, was a sportsman turned evangelist with a gentle Irish sense of humour and complete dedication to his religious mission in life.

Monty's mother Maud was the daughter of a famous Victorian writer and preacher. 'There was no question about it, a great deal of my brother's determination and his decisive opinions and indeed his domination sprang entirely from her,' Monty's brother Brian related. 'Our mother was an extremely strong-minded person. It was mother who controlled the entire finances of the family. She dictated as to what clothes we were to wear and in my case it was always somebody else's trousers.'

forgiven you".

"The Lord may have forgiven you – but I have not!" came a voice from the chapel door, where Monty's mother was standing. He was led away for caning.

'I was the bad boy of the family, the rebellious one, and as a result I learnt early to stand or fall on my own. She (my mother) made me afraid of her when I was a child and a young boy...There was an absence of affectionate understanding of the problems facing the young. My father got bullied a good deal by my mother and she could always make him do what she wanted.'

Thus wrote Monty some sixty years later. The scars of childhood never really healed – and if one wishes to understand the awkward, insubordinate commander of later years, one must undoubtedly seek the origins in the fierce clash of wills between mother and son in the colonial atmosphere of late Victorian Tasmania.

In 1901 when Monty was thirteen, his father was summoned back to London to become the chief administrator of the Anglican missionary movement.

Monty and his elder brother, Donald, were sent to St Paul's public school. Donald had obtained a scholarship and, like his father, would go to Cambridge, becoming a distinguished lawyer in Canada. For the black sheep of the family, however, there were no such expectations. On his first day at St Paul's Monty joined Army Class 'C' – to the consternation of the Bishop, who hoped Bernard would one day enter the Church.

Such a hope does not say much for Bishop Montgomery's understanding of his son's fundamentally pugnacious character. Yet in one way the Bishop was right. In the years ahead Monty would become, without question, the outstanding military evangelist of the twentieth century: a man whose missionary zeal and simple doctrines of war were to take him to the top of his profession.

Monty's childhood: Hobart, Tasmania, where Monty spent his childhood years.

Nestling beneath Mount Wellington and the Hartz Mountains, Hobart was a neat, country town with streets that led down to a harbour filled with steamers, clippers, schooners and coastal luggers.

The Montgomery children were educated by private tutors sent from England and punished if they lapsed into local dialect. Nevertheless the colonial atmosphere – with ample opportunity for pony-riding, fishing, picnicking and mountain walking – was to have a profound impact on Monty's character. Far from being the typical 'Limey' of American caricature, Monty would always remain outrageously un-English, with an Australian bravado and no-nonsense approach to life.

Monty, aged 9, in the garden in Hobart, in characteristic pose. 'My childhood was unhappy. This was due to a clash of wills between my mother and myself,' he later wrote. 'My early life was a series of fierce battles, from which my mother invariably emerged the victor.'

'There were definite rules for us children; these had to be obeyed; disobedience brought swift punishment. A less rigid discipline, and more affectionate understanding, might have wrought better, certainly different results in me. My brothers and sisters were not so difficult; they were more amenable to the régime and gave no trouble.'

Monty the rebel had been born.

The Turning Point

n due course Monty passed into the Royal Military College, Sandhurst and was quickly promoted Lance-Corporal Cadet for his leadership qualities, but he was soon in serious trouble. Gang warfare had become part and parcel of the Sandhurst tradition. Leading his own company of cadets, armed with a poker, Monty roasted a fellow cadet's backside in the manner of Tom Brown's Schooldays. The badly burned victim was hospitalised. Monty was about to be dismissed from Sandhurst when Maud Montgomery intervened.

It is unlikely that Maud acted out of love for Monty, since patently she did not love this most unloveable boy, but she wished to spare her husband, the Bishop, from scandal. She therefore travelled post haste to see the Commandant in person. She was a handsome, determined lady. She got her way. Stripped of his Lance-Corporal's stripe, Monty was reprieved.

For Monty this was a turning point in his life. He had sought, like a child, to attract maximum attention by his outrageous behaviour. He had succeeded, but come perilously close to ruining his future military career. From now on he would attempt to gain his mother's attention not by defiance but by distinction.

Cadet B.L. Montgomery passed out 36th in order of merit from Sandhurst. This was an excellent result considering that he was not in any way bookish, but unfortunately it was not high enough to permit him entry into the coveted Indian Army, where an officer could live on his pay. Monty therefore applied for a commission in an English regiment which had a battalion fighting in Northern India and Afghanistan: the Royal Warwickshire Regiment. There his pay would be sufficient to maintain an officer's way of life.

On 12 December 1908, Second Lieutenant B.L. Montgomery joined the 1st Battalion, The Royal Warwickshire Regiment, stationed in Peshawar. He arrived too late for the Bazaar Valley and Mohmand punitive expeditions. Instead, he devoted himself to signalling and reconnaissance – aspects of soldiering which he would make hallmarks of his military command in later years.

Monty's school holidays had always been spent at Moville, near Londonderry, where the Bishop had inherited large Montgomery estates. This and his childhood experience of the hills and outback in Tasmania, gave Monty great physical confidence outdoors.

On the Himalayan frontier he rode, hunted and learned the minor skills of soldiering. What he did not receive, as he later recorded, was the remotest grounding in war as it might be fought in modern-day Europe.

When the Royal Warwickshires moved in 1910 to Bombay – 'the sloth belt' – Monty refused to be slothful. He became Assistant Adjutant and Battalion Games Officer, but his argumentativeness annoyed his superiors.

On one occasion, for instance, he was ordered to field a mediocre team to play a friendly football match against the visiting German battleship *Gneisenau* - carrying the German Crown Prince. Far from fielding mediocrities, Monty chose his very best players. The Germans were trounced 40 – nil.

To the remonstrations of the battalion adjutant, Monty retorted unrepentantly: "Oh, I wasn't taking any chances with those bastards!"

Tactlessness, then, was engrained in Monty's self-willed character. He also visited a Bombay brothel, an experience that would prove of great significance later in his attitude towards 'horizontal refreshment' for the men under his command. In the main, though, he himself showed no interest in the fairer sex or in matrimony – particularly on a subaltern's pay.

Returning to England in 1912, Monty lost his foreign service allowance. He had saved diligently however. He had also become a fanatical motorist, and so in England he purchased a motor car, intending to drive to Ireland to stay with his parents in the summer of 1914.

Leave, however, was not granted. As the Austro-Hungarian crisis deepened, the prospect of war with Germany appeared inevitable.

Monty's battalion was soon posted from Folkestone to the Thames estuary to repel a possible German landing, thence to the north-east coast near York to face a second Saxon invasion. War had already been declared, and on 22 August 1914 the 1st Battalion, the Royal Warwickshire Regiment ended its futile perambulations around England. It embarked for France and battle.

Monty, training fifty hand-picked men from his battalion as reconnaissance Scouts, on the North-West Frontier of India, 1909. 'Looking back, I would put this period as the time when it was becoming apparent to me that to succeed one must master one's profession,' Monty wrote.

Custom dictated otherwise, however. 'The basic trouble was a beastly climate and the absence of contact with Europe,' Monty wrote. 'An expression heard frequently was that so-and-so was a "good mixer"... It soon appeared to me that a good mixer was a man who had never been known to refuse a drink... There did seem to me to be something lacking in the whole business... It was not fashionable to study war and we were not allowed to talk about our profession in the Officers' Mess.'

Transferred with his regiment to the Bombay 'sloth belt', Monty refused to be slothful. He passed out top with distinction in the Army Signals examination and made history in the battalion as Sports Officer – fielding his entire prize-winning football eleven in order to trounce a visiting team from the German battleship *Gneisenau*, against his Colonel's wishes.

'I was amazed sometimes at Monty's energy and unabated keenness,' wrote a colleague, 'but truth to tell he was sometimes a little argumentative and did not always do as he was told.'

The Fog of War

Lieutenant Bernard Montgomery's infantry battalion was marched straight from Boulogne into the Battle of Mons, the great German right-wheel by which its armies, having overrun most of Belgium, hoped to out-flank Paris.

His first experience of war was salutary. Communications were as bad as in Napoleonic days. The higher British commanders were torn between the desire to give battle and to withdraw in good order. Savage casualties were the inevitable result. Montgomery was ordered into battle at the head of his platoon armed only with a sword. Fortunately, standing only 5' 9", he tripped over his scabbard, while all around him his colleagues and men fell 'like ninepins', as he wrote subsequently to his mother. German Maxim machine guns decimated a British battalion launched into battle without reconnaissance, tactical siting, or plan of attack. Worse still the Battalion Colonel then ran away and surrendered to the enemy, leaving the survivors of the battle – including Monty – to make their way back, hiding by day and marching by night through the advancing German lines.

The Commander of the British Expeditionary Force wished to withdraw his army from the campaign altogether, but Field Marshal Kitchener refused permission. The French 6th Army counterattacked, the German encirclement of Paris was postponed, and the BEF was put back into the Allied line near Ypres as part of the October 'race to the sea'. Commanding a company of survivors and reinforcements from Britain, Monty once again led an infantry charge, this time towards the village of Meteren. This successful action earned him the coveted Distinguished Service Order, and restored the good name of the battalion. It was, however, Monty's downfall, for in the aftermath of the charge a German sniper shot Captain Montgomery (promoted that day) through the lung. One of his men rushed forward to dress the wound, but was killed outright, falling over Monty's body and protecting it from further sniper shots. For three further hours Monty lay bleeding until at nightfall a stretcher party recovered his body. A grave had been dug at the field dressing station but evidence of life was detected and he was sent back unconscious to England by hospital train.

Although the bullet had passed straight through his chest, the wound was mercifully clean, and the lung healed sufficiently for Monty to be given a job in 1915 as a Brigade-Major charged with raising a brigade of Lancashire infantrymen, nicknamed 'Bantams' because of their short stature. In order to make successful soldiers out of untrained civilians, Monty had now to put himself into the hearts and minds of the men, to become a teacher and organiser. This for Monty was one of the great lessons of World War I.

By 1916 Montgomery was back in action on the Western Front. His days as a front-line fighting soldier, however, were over. For the rest of the war he would serve as a staff officer at brigade, division and Corps head-quarters in the field.

Monty had never attended a staff school, nor received any instruction in higher tactics or training. His experiences at the battles of the Somme – where in eight days almost one in five of the men in the brigade became casualties – Arras, Passchendaele, the Lys and Amiens, taught him the value of clear orders, good communications and realistic objectives and also the limits of human endurance. Courage alone was not enough. 'The Canadians,' he wrote to his mother in November 1917, having witnessed their incredible gallantry at Passchendaele, 'are a queer crowd…I was disappointed in them. At plain, straightforward fighting they are magnificent, but they are narrow-minded and lack soldierly instincts…They forget that the whole art of war is to gain your

Monty (right of picture) back in France as a Staff Officer in 1916, with his brother Donald (left of picture) who was serving with the Canadian Corps. Monty had been severely wounded in 1914. His Brigadier wrote to Monty's father that he had 'the very highest opinion of him. He is equally good at Administration as at Training of Troops. He ought to have a brilliant future in the Army, and rise to high rank.'

Monty's opinion of his Brigadier was characteristic: 'My brigadier was an old retired officer – a very nice person but quite useless, and it would be true to say that I really ran the Brigade, and they all knew it.'

objective with as little loss as possible.'

Upon this doctrine, Monty was to base his whole approach to war: not heroics or glory-seeking, but the plain, unromantic task of assessing one's objectives and ensuring, by rehearsal and clear orders, that they could be realized with the minimum loss of human life.

There was one further development. In four years Monty rose from Lieutenant to Lieutenant-Colonel, as Chief of Staff of a division numbering 15,000 men. War suited him, he found. No teacher at St Paul's School or Sandhurst had ever prophesied a grand career for Bernard Montgomery, yet it was in the quality of his concise, logical and relentlessly simplifying mind that Montgomery made his reputation in World War 1. His first brigadier predicted a 'brilliant future in the Army'. Everything

Monty wrote during the war was stamped with conviction from movement order to training instructions and battle plans. In the fog of war he found he possessed the pearl of military talents: clarity.

In the town of Lille on 28 October 1918 Lt-Colonel Bernard Montgomery triumphantly 'rode with the general at the head of the Division till we reached the Grande Place, then we got off our horses and stood with the Mayor while the troops marched past; it took 2½ hours for them to go by... The whole Division with all its transport etc takes up 14 miles of road!'

Behind Montgomery stood the British Minister of Munitions, Mr Winston Churchill, but they were not introduced, and it would be another 21 years before they would be: in the aftermath of the great German battle of revenge, the Battle of France 1940.

Chief-of-Staff of a division and in the temporary rank of Lt- Colonel, Monty watches his men parade at Lille in October 1914. 'One is gaining wonderful experience in this advance. As Chief- of-Staff I have to work out plans in detail for the operations. . . The day generally commences with an attack at dawn, after which we continue to work slowly forward all day; then another organized attack is arranged for the next morning to carry us forward again, and so on. It means little sleep and continuous work; at night guns have to be moved forward, communications arranged, food and ammunition got up, etc. etc.

'The heads of the various branches are all Lt-Colonels, older and senior in rank (but not in position as I am Chief-of-Staff) to me and one is a Brigadier-General. But we all work in very well together and they do what I tell them like lambs.'

Behind Monty sits the Minister of Munitions in the British Government, Mr Winston Churchill.

Learning the Lessons

Within months of Germany's defeat in November 1918, Lt-Colonel Montgomery had reverted to his substantive rank of Captain, with the assurance of accelerated promotion to Major once a vacancy occured. Unfortunately, after swingeing Government cuts in the Services in the early 1920's, the prospects for such promotion looked long and drawn-out.

Having survived the carnage of World War 1, Monty wished to attend the Army's Staff College, Camberley. Not finding his name on the list of students accepted in 1919, he bearded the Commander-in-Chief of the British Army of Occupation, in Cologne, during a tennis match, little imagining he himself would become Commander-in-Chief of such an Army only 25 years later.

Field-Marshal Robertson had risen from the rank of Private, and still dropped his H's. Monty appealed to him for a chance to study the lessons of the war properly. Impressed, Robertson saw to it that Montgomery's name was added to the next Camberley list.

Monty's zeal soon earned him black marks in an Army tired of war and intent on reviving the art of polo. At Camberley in 1920 it was considered a punishment to have to sit beside Montgomery at breakfast. From early morning to the evening Monty questioned the syllabus and the lessons being taught. His punishment was to be sent, in 1921, to southern Ireland as a Brigade-Major. In due course he became responsible for marshalling and giving out orders to some nine British battalions in his Brigade during the Troubles. His cousin was assassinated in Dublin, and there were 'terrorist' outrages which taxed the patience of the men almost beyond endurance. 'We have to be very careful as a false step would be a match that would set

the whole country ablaze,' Monty wrote to his father from Cork in 1922. Monty managed the embarcation of the last of his troops in May of that year without further bloodshed. He had learned great lessons in France and Flanders about the nature of modern, full-scale war. In Ireland he had learned a different reality: that in a smaller, guerrilla war, a nation as democratic and fundamentally decent as the British could not quell a genuinely nationalist uprising for ever.

'My own view is that to win a war of that sort you must be ruthless; Oliver Cromwell, or the Germans, would have settled it in a very short time. Nowadays public opinion precludes such methods. The nation would never allow it, and the politicians would lose their jobs if they sanctioned it...The only way therefore was to give them (the Irish) some form of self-government, and let them squash the rebellion themselves.'

Profound realism, then, tempered Monty's energetic pursuit of his career. He was not attracted by modernism for modernism's sake. What he wanted to do was to blow away the fog of war, to clarify the principles of battle: preparation, training, battle planning, rehearsal and the responsiblity of senior officers to put their men into battle with a good chance of success. Consigned to a backwater as an officer in a Territorial division in York, Montgomery tirelessly wrote pamphlets on war and on battle training for his part-time charges, as well as essays on the history of tactics for his regimental journal. Despite his awkward, harrying personality, it was not altogether unsurprising when, in 1924, Montgomery was posted to the Staff College, Camberley as an Instructor, with the rank of Lieutenant-Colonel. The erstwhile 'dud' of St Paul's School had become himself a teacher of a stature.

First, however, Montgomery took

stock of his life in the relentlessly logical way that had become his hallmark. He wished to command, not simply to teach command. But to command his battalion, convention demanded that he have wife. He therefore decided that he would be a mysogonist no longer. He was thirty-seven. It was time to seek a bride.

The 'Troubles' in Ireland, 1921. Here, Monty's Brigadier interrogates IRA 'suspects' rounded up during an anti-terrorist drive near Cork. Monty, the Brigade-Major, stands on extreme right. 'A little tiger for work, and by Jove you have to jump when he gives you any order!' a subordinate described him.

'In many ways this was far worse than the Great War. . .such a war is thoroughly bad for officers and men; it tends to lower their standards of decency and chivalry, and I was glad when it was over,' Monty recorded.

Monty the Suitor

Bernard Montgomery first saw the beautiful 17-year-old Betty Anderson in the ballroom of a hotel in Dinard, where he was staying on a spring golfing holiday with his battalion Colonel. She was there with her parents, on furlough from the Indian Political Service. Monty seized her hand, rushed her onto the floor, and at the end of the first dance announced that he was going to marry her!

'I thought really quite truthfully I'd met someone who was just a bit loopy,' Betty later recalled. 'Anyway, he seemed awfully old to me – I mean, seventeen and thirty-seven was quite a big gap.'

Monty, unwilling to face defeat even afer such a reckless and unreconnoitred attack, resorted to an alternative strategy: he spoke to Betty's parents. Impressed by his future prospects in the army, they urged their daughter to reconsider. A compromise was agreed: each day Betty and Bernard would go for a walk by the sea to get to know one another.

Betty was studying music, having turned down offers to become a fashion model. She found Major Montgomery's conversation limited. He was clearly obsessed with matters military, even illustrating his account of war and military manoeuvres by drawing in the sand. However talented a teacher, it was clear that such lecturing was not the way to a young girl's heart. At the end of a week Betty put an end to the experiment. 'I said, "I'm terribly sorry but I've not changed my mind at all." We said goodbye, and that was the end of that.'

It was not, unfortunately. At the end of 1925 the Camberley instructor — now a Lieutenant-Colonel – was once again in pursuit. He had heard that Betty and her parents, together with a party of other Indian Civil Servants, were skiing in Switzerland, in the Wildstrubel Hotel in the village of Lenk. To Betty's consternation, her rejected suitor stood before her, threatening to wreck her holiday.

Betty was furious, and Monty quickly saw that his quest was doomed. He promised not to intrude on her holiday, and busied himself on the slopes. It had been his first attempt to loose himself from his emotional bondage to his mother, and it had failed. He sought consolation by teaching John and Richard Carver, the sons of another member of the party, to ski. The boys liked him. Monty was energetic and fun, having a schoolboyish sort of humour. It never occurred to them that their widowed mother, a painter, might be attracted by the avuncular, military sportsman, until, months later, they were asked if they would like to return to Lenk for another skiing holiday the following Christmas.

Once again the energetic Colonel was there. He began to skate with their mother on the rink and share meals with them. Their mother had been widowed for ten years, and they themselves had never really known their father, who had been killed at the Dardanelles in the Great War. Events seemed to take a slow but inevitable course: a friendship which deepened into love.

Betty Carver was the same age as Monty. Her brother, Patrick Hobart, was also a Colonel in the army, a brilliant proponent of the tank. Betty wasn't beautiful, but she had intelligence, a womanly, Irish charm and unusual artistic talent. She had studied art at the Slade, she mixed with bohemians, artists and writers of the day, from Augustus John to Arnold Bennett. Sensitive and perceptive, she could see that her boys were reaching an age when they needed a father's guidance. Others might mock Monty for his eccentricity, his devotion to the art and teaching of soldiering at a time when the very word war was anathema. But Betty Carver was no ordinary woman. Whatever her bohemian friends might say,

Monty in 1926, having been appointed an Instructor at the Army's Staff College in Camberley. 'He reached the conclusion that he ought to get married. He used to get these ideas,' Monty's brother Brian recalled.

'He first tried to get married to a very young girl. Well

that didn't work out at all – he asked her to marry him, but it didn't work out, which was a fortunate thing. But then he met, during a winter holiday in Switzerland, the widow of an officer who'd been killed in World War One, a sapper. And he found her to be exactly the girl for him.'

Betty Anderson, the beautiful 17-year-old débutante to whom Monty proposed in 1925, on holiday in France. Betty Anderson's father worked in the Indian Political Service, but had served in the army and was convinced that Monty would 'go far'. Betty Anderson found the attentions of the 37-year-old bachelor tedious, and rejected him outright, to the disappointment of her parents.

Despite her refusal of his proposal, Monty followed Betty Anderson to Lenk the following Christmas.

Monty dressed as Napoleon, at the Wildstrubel Hotel Fancy Dress Ball, Christmas 1925. 'My friends of course thought it was hilariously funny that I should have been asked to get married to that old man – double my age!' recalled Betty Anderson. 'He always used to say to me; "Call me Bernard," but I never called him anything but Monty. Anyway, I said to these friends of mine: "Look, what am I going to do? I simply must make him see I cannot marry him."

'There was going to be a fancy dress dance at the hotel. I said, "I know what I'll do, I'll go as a newspaper boy"! So I blackened my face and put on trousers and tucked my hair under my cap and behaved like an idiot, shouting out in cockney "Paper!" all evening. He went, as you can guess, as Napoleon!'

Monty, Junior Instructor at the Staff College, Camberley 1926. 'He taught us tactics and battlefield leadership,' recalled one of his students sixty years later.

'He was a brilliant teacher. . .very clear, very concise; left you in no doubt what the situation was. I was spokesman for my syndicate on a tactical exercise and Monty was Instructor in charge of us. I had to give our solution. I started off thinking I had a very good solution. After I had gone a little way, Monty said: "That's interesting!" Now that was a warning shot! But he said, "Well, continue and finish." So I finished. "Well, Harding, I am sure you and your syndicate have given a lot of thought and discussion to this problem, but all I can say is that your solution could have ended only one way; a scene of intense military confusion!"

'Any success that I may have had in my military career was almost entirely due to what I was taught by him at the Staff College' – Field-Marshal Lord Harding, 1986.

Betty Carver, at the time when Monty married her, in 1927. 'She already had two sons by her first marriage and he was determined to marry her. This was interesting because her whole background was something quite strange to him,' Brian Montgomery described. 'She was a very cultured person. She painted, she was a sculptor. She was extremely well read and she had a knowledge of the arts which was certainly very much superior to his own.

'She always made him see the funny side of things. If he was upset, she would see it and make him laugh, and only she could do that. She was a woman of great character, very charming, and it's a tragedy the marriage didn't continue, for she was successful at rubbing off those sharp edges from his character, which appeared to some people to be so strange.'

war and human conflict were facts of life. Monty's mission, to instruct a cadre of the British Army capable of conducting modern war successfully and with the minimum loss of life, seemed to Betty Carver a noble aim. In Bernard Montgomery Betty recognized the spirit of genius: a man possessed with the infinite capacity for taking pains, yet imbued with a desire to simplify the mechanics of war, to reduce the complexity of a modern army by ruthlessly clear priorities, and by simple tenets. She had met him at the very moment in his career when he was formulating his philosophy of war, in many eyes the finest tactical teacher the Staff College had ever known. Many of his students would become distinguished commanders in the subsequent World War – Alexander, Dempsey, Nye, Harding, Templer, Gale, Kennedy, McCreery to name but a few – and had fate ruled Monty out for active service in World War II, which it very nearly did, Monty would have gone down in British military history as the finest teacher of tactics of his generation.

Betty Carver, despite her bohemian links, was aware of this. Though his manner was eccentric, even a bit 'loopy', and though his bossiness and mania for tidiness did not make him a conventionally attractive figure, Betty saw beneath the awkward surface, understanding the thirty-nine year old somewhat emotionally retarded adult, still tormented by his need to prove himself to his tyrannical mother. She responded with trust, understanding and affection, and in the spring of 1927, while on a visit to John Carver's school sports day at Charterhouse, the matter of their future came to a head.

People had begun to talk, Betty said; perhaps it would be better if they did not see each other for a while. Nonsense, replied Monty, he loved her. Betty burst into tears; and they became engaged to be married. Monty the inveterate bachelor — the man who had declared 'You can't make a good soldier and a good husband' – was to be married.

A Married Man

The marriage between Lt-Colonel Bernard Montgomery and Mrs Betty Carver was held at Chiswick Parish Church on 27 July 1927. Monty's father, Bishop Montgomery, took the service, assisted by Monty's brother Colin, who had become a clergyman. Monty's brother Brian, who had gone into the army, was best man.

The family expected a great reception after the church ceremony; some hoped for drink. But to their consternation, Monty pushed Betty into his car and drove away, leaving the family speechless on the church steps.

This was to be Monty's attitude for the rest of his life. Nearing 40, he had proved himself within his profession. Now he wished to prove himself as a husband and as a father, to cast off the emotional chains binding him to his mother and to his family. Henceforth he would be his own boss, answerable not to his mother but to himself – and to Betty.

Monty's love for his wife is perhaps the most touching aspect of this strange, dedicated and somewhat bullying soldier. He ran the household, even engaging the servants. The energetic staff officer in him could not bear disorder or untidiness, while the commander in him rapped out orders unceasingly. Yet he was under no illusion: his new-found happiness, discovered so late in life, was wholly due to Betty. *In camera*, he always deferred to her. Betty had talents which the sharp-nosed Lieutenant-Colonel would never aspire to: intuitive, sensitive, artistically gifted, she opened his eyes to another world. It was not a world in which Monty would ever 'fit' but it increased Monty's receptivity to new ideas and made him recognize the talent that existed outside the army: talent which could one day be marshalled in a largely civilian army, with officers and men drawn from all walks of life. That Monty would be able to harness such talent and would understand the aspirations of civilian soldiers and their wives – important ingredients in the world-historical figure Monty would become – undoubtedly owed much to his marriage to Betty. Monty's own domain remained the study and practice of war, but through his marriage Monty the obsessive soldier was introduced to the worlds of art, of writing, of politics (through Betty's friend the M.P. and writer A.P. Herbert) and industry. His horizons were broadening, and it was no surprise when, in 1928, he was asked by the War Office to rewrite the army's *Infantry Training Manual*.

As a staff officer Monty's future was now assured. But Monty's ambition was to command an army. To do this he had to follow the prescribed army route: command of a battalion, then a brigade, a division, a Corps...Each step was littered with the shattered hopes of ambitious men. Liddell-Hart had been cast out of the army as a junior Captain, forced to become a hack journalist. 'Bony' Fuller, another proponent of armoured warfare, was also forced to resign, never being offered battalion command.

Though he aroused strong feelings in the army by his ruthless professionalism, Monty's marriage undoubtedly improved his prospects. In 1929 he was made Second-in-Command of the 1st Battalion of the Royal Warwickshire Regiment and finally, on 17 January 1931, Lt-Colonel B.L. Montgomery set sail for the Holy Land as Commanding Officer of the battalion. He was waved off by his father, the saintly Bishop, whom he would never see again.

Monty was quite certain there would be another war. The regular army and its volunteer reserve, the Territorials, would have to be trained as the cadre of a conscript, national army. Whether in Britain or abroad, officers and men must therefore use their time profitably in the study and rehearsal of their future role in

battle: and in Palestine in 1931 and Egypt from 1931 to 1933 Monty sought to rehearse his battalion as an army in miniature. Ceremonial drill was abandoned entirely. While performing the tasks of an occupying or guardian military power, Monty concentrated on battle training and manoeuvres. To fight by day and move by night was Monty's ambition, and to achieve this the battalion must rehearse until navigation and movement became second-nature to the units.

Thereafter tactical disposition, good communications and well-practised co-operation with other arms – machine guns, engineers, artillery and armour – were the order of the day. Monty's energy and ambitions for the battalion were not always popular among his superiors – particularly when Monty defied Brigade Headquarters and took the battalion into the Egyptian desert on exercises, making the men march when Brigade HQ withheld transport!

Monty, parades his battalion, encamped beneath the pyramids, Egypt, 1932. 'The finest trainer of troops I've ever met in my life,' one of his company commanders recalled. 'Mark you, there were COs I had more affection for, let's be quite honest!'

'His great thing of course was training by night. The soldier, he'd say, *must* be trained to exercise his skills in the dark, especially with machine-guns and support guns.'

'It is a positive pleasure to watch him commanding his unit on manoeuvres,' wrote his Brigadier in Alexandria – but he was glad to see the back of Monty.

Monty and his wife Betty in Jerusalem, 1931: a city which, given Monty's religious upbringing, made a profound impression: 'an eastern city of 1000 years ago or more; little narrow streets, donkeys camels and humans all jostling each other, brilliant colours in the bazaars, and many smells. Parts of the wall are of Herod's time. I saw on Sunday the entrance gate to Pilate's hall, and the paved street up which Jesus walked with his Cross. . . The view from the Mt of Olives across the garden of Gethsemane towards Jerusalem is wonderful.'

In the view of Monty's brother Brian and his sister Winsome, this was the happiest time of Monty's life. He took Betty to Petra, Jerash, Damascus and Baalbec: 'It had never seemed possible that such love and affection could exist. We went everywhere, and did everything together.'

If Monty infuriated his superiors, he was devoted to the welfare of his men. He instituted promotion by merit rather than length of service, and took the view that hard work ought to be rewarded by sports, concert parties and leave. Aware that the ladies of Alexandria were an attraction that could not be denied men on 6-year overseas service, Monty set up a battalion brothel, inspected regularly by the battalion medical officer. Moreover, despite his reputation as a martinet, the scourge of idlers and amateurs, he could be understanding too. One of his company commanders faced possible court-martial for drink and women. Monty dismissed the charges on condition that the officer reformed. If he felt he could not control his urges, he was to contact Monty. One evening, as Monty was dining with his wife, the telephone rang. The officer explained that he had done his best to reform, but that the time had come when he simply must have a woman. 'All right,' answered Monty, 'But just one, mind!'

Such stories soon began to circulate among the regiments, creating a Monty legend: a fanatical trainer, with a mission to prepare the British army for future war, at a time when Britain's empire seemed secure and Europe was at peace, a man capable of the grossest acts of insubordination, yet dedicated to the welfare of his men.

'He is clever, energetic, ambitious and a very gifted instructor,' the area commander in the Middle East wrote in Monty's personal report in 1932. 'But if he is to do himself full justice in the higher positions to which his gifts should entitle him, he must cultivate tact, tolerance, and discretion.'

Monty was now in his forties. He was offered two staff appointments but turned them down. 'At the end of the year I shall take this battalion to India. I shall

then become a brigadier and after that I shall take command of a division, ending up as CIGS [head of the British Army],' he explained to one of his officers.

Few men have ever been as clear about their goal in life or as dedicated in achieving it as Monty. What he did not take into account was his area commander's warning that his military talents alone would not assure the attainment of high command. Promotion in peacetime is a slow, laborious and frustrating ascent, requiring tact and discretion, and when Monty duly took his battalion to India at the end of 1933 it looked for a time as if his star had reached its zenith. Hitler had taken power in Germany, but no area commander in Britain seemed anxious to have Monty back as a brigadier. Lt-Colonel B.L. Montgomery was stuck, in the 'sloth belt' of India.

The Holy Land, 1931, with his son David. In addition to being Colonel of the 1st Battalion, The Royal Warwickshire Regiment, Monty commanded all troops stationed in Palestine, as well as maintaining relations with foreign forces stationed in Syria, Transjordan and the Lebanon. 'It was just his cup of tea,' his stepson recalled later. 'He was in his element; in fact he got definite ideas of grandeur. I wanted to go down to Egypt, so he wrote in his own fair hand, across a full page, in my passport: "On Duty in Egypt", signed B.L. Montgomery. He thought that was good enough – that you could go round the world on his signature!'

The Sloth Belt

General Sir George Jeffries was Commander-in-Chief in southern India when the 1st Battalion of the Royal Warwickshire Regiment arrived in Poona in January 1931. No sooner were they settled in than there were fireworks of a personal kind. Jeffries was a stickler for ceremonial drill; Monty was not. The story goes that Jeffries ordered the battalion to parade on the Poona race course, with Monty at its head.

"Colonel, you are seven paces too far to the left!" roared Jeffries. Monty turned round in his saddle. "Battalion: seven paces to the right!"

Jeffries and Monty were on collision course. When Jeffries ordered armed church parades on Sundays, Monty deliberately queried the order, asking against what threat he was to dispose his

the next step in his military ascent, but no post had been offered him. To remain as Lieutenant-Colonel under Jeffries would result in downfall. Though it was a side-step, the post in Quetta would give Monty a further chance to refine his doctrine of command in modern war, and to put it over to many hundreds of students.

Monty was now 47; by the time he completed three years tenure at Quetta he would be almost 50. Often, in the course of his lectures, Monty would warn his students that war with Germany was inevitable, but that he himself might not survive in the service long enough to fight again. His contemporaries, such as Auchinleck, even his juniors such as Alexander and O'Connor, were already serving as Brigadiers in action on the North-West frontier. Monty was slipping behind. He exhorted his Quetta charges not to neglect the opportunity to study

Quetta, 1936. Betty Montgomery gives the tennis prizes at the Staff College, Quetta. Monty, behind the sofa, applauds. 'She was dark and vivacious, always cheerful and frequently laughing,' recalled one student. 'Much of a height and age as Monty; she dressed soberly in the fashion of the day, but not to draw attention by being eccentric in any way; always attractively turned out. . . They were devoted to one another and didn't mind showing it.'

troops — the Germans?

Before Jeffries could sack Monty for insubordination, providence came to Monty's assistance, in the form of a cable from Simla, the summer GHQ of the Indian Army. It offered Monty a senior Instructorship at the Staff College, Quetta, with promotion to full Colonel.

At first, Monty was hesitant. He had set his eyes upon Brigade command as

their profession in view of the coming war. 'Remember it will be *your* show,' he warned – 'and you must now get on with the business of making yourselves professionals in your chosen profession – because we only have the time it takes Germany to become what she considers to be sufficiently re-armed.'

Professionalism had become Monty's watchword. While other officers and military writers were obsessed by the new firepower and mobility promised by the tank, Monty addressed himself to what he saw as the *real* problem: how to defeat an enemy who wishes to deprive you of your mobility. In Monty's view it could be achieved not by gimmicks but by a cold-blooded professionalism: first-class staff work, realistic planning, good communications, rehearsal not only of the soldiery but of the 'bureaucracy' of command. Commanders and staff must

'know their stuff': the interaction of infantry, artillery, engineers, tanks and the air force. 'There's no doubt we all felt immensely privileged to be taught the higher aspects of our profession by someone of Monty's calibre,' one student – who became a full General – later recalled. 'The whole instructing staff was under his charge, and I think they learned as much from Monty as we students did.'

But Monty was learning too. He wore a distinctive, old-fashioned white

Monty playing soldiers with his son David, Staff College, Quetta, 1935 where Monty was Chief Instructor. It was at Quetta that Monty's vision of tactics and command in modern war crystallized.

'Any future C-in-C has got to be well-known, not only to the soldiers, but to their wives and mothers,' he declared to his students. 'A fine trainer and a convincing teacher,' the Commandant reported, but Monty's ambition to become a general in the field seemed blighted by Britain's small peacetime army and Monty's own professionalism, which frightened his superiors.

topee on exercises. When ragged by one student, Monty retorted that there was nothing embarrassing in the wearing of unusual hats: "Winston Churchill always goes in for unusual hats – so do I." He learned to speak without notes; and within a year the Commandant was urgently recommending him for promotion to Brigadier either on the staff or in command of a Brigade.

The years passed, however, and no post was offered to Monty. In March 1936 Hitler invaded the Rhineland. In May Mussolini conquered Abyssinia. In the summer German and Italian forces were sent to fight in Spain. Finally, in February 1937 the War Office cabled Monty to offer him command of the 9th Infantry Brigade at Portsmouth, which would become vacant on 5 August 1937.

Monty and Betty were delighted. Betty had given birth to a son, David, in 1928 and the years of travelling – to Palestine, Egypt and India – had eventually necessitated sending David back to England. Now the family would be together again.

Monty had enjoyed ten happy years of marriage. 'We went everywhere and did everything together,' Monty later wrote. 'It had never before seemed possible that such love and affection could exist.'

In England, in June and July 1937, Monty had two months leave. He and Betty toured the Lake District. Then Monty sent Betty to a hotel in Burnham-on-Sea with his eight-year-old son David, while he took his new infantry Brigade on manoeuvres on Salisbury Plain.

These manoeuvres were of crucial importance to Brigadier B.L. Montgomery, for they would demonstrate whether he was simply an outstanding teacher or whether he had it in him to command large forces in action. His Commandant in Quetta had stated, in his final report, that Monty was 'fitted now for promotion to Major-General'. The manoeuvres on Salisbury Plain would be a test of that assertion.

With his 4,000 troops, including Territorial units, under canvas, Brigadier Montgomery took command of 9th Infantry Brigade in August 1937. But Monty was not the only one on trial. The manoeuvres he conducted with aplomb outclassed the 'enemy' brigade. But on the sands of Burnham-on-Sea Monty's wife Betty was stung by an insect. Her leg swelled and she was moved into the little local cottage hospital. There she began the long, painful struggle for her life.

Monty, mounted, outside his bungalow in Quetta, 1934. 'All those who have served with Colonel Montgomery will regret that the Regiment is to lose an officer who has done so much to instill into all ranks the modern theory of war,' the Royal Warwickshire regimental magazine recorded when Monty was posted to the Staff College, Quetta. In fact 'the senior officers, they didn't like him,' his successor recorded. 'Monty thought they were a lot of dug-ins. . . The truth is, there wasn't enough for Monty to do, commanding a battalion. Not in Poona – Poona was a very fashionable social place – and Monty didn't care for that much.'

Monty now reverted to being a teacher.

Betty's Death

n the drama of the mock battle on Salisbury Plain, and his desire to imprint his personality and military doctrine upon his new brigade, Monty had neglected Betty, not taking seriously a seemingly minor infection. Then, as the true gravity of her condition became clear to him, he wished to have her moved to the large hospital at Portsmouth. 'Poor Monty – his cut and dried plans miscarry,' wrote Betty's cousin, the only person Monty would allow to nurse and be with her. 'He had 'time-tabled' that she was to be moved to Portsmouth last week, then it was to be today…Monty, I fear, has still to learn that in serious illness things do not work out according to plan like ordering an advance at dawn!'

Betty's condition worsened relentlessly. Transfer to Portsmouth was ruled out. Eventually the doctor recommended amputation. Monty agreed. Betty would have an artificial limb, more domestic help; he himself would learn to do more things for her…

The amputation did no good, however. On 19th October 1937 Betty died in Monty's arms.

For two days Monty was distraught, unable to take in the tragedy. No one had ever seen him in such a state. He would allow no one to be present at the funeral in Burnham-on-Sea, save his Brigade-Major and an army driver. No member of Monty's or Betty's family was invited. It was as if Monty wished no witness to his grief, his loss of self-control. All his life, since childhood, he had sought to be in control of his destiny, to defeat his mother's emotional stranglehold. Betty had enabled him to escape from Maud's chains to find unexpected happiness and an ever-deepening public mission to prepare himself and his subordinates for the coming war. Being considered eccentric and talented, but not mad, he had successfully survived the transition from Major to Colonel to Brigadier. The

'loopy' suitor had become an adoring husband, a loving father, a devoted step-father. Yet at the very moment when Monty seemed poised to achieve high command, his reports that autumn all extolling his 'quick brain and clear head', his 'powers of leadership' and military 'vision', fate dictated that he lose his wife.

Monty left the graveside alone, refusing to travel back with his Brigade-Major in the staff car. He had broken down by the grave, and the Brigade-Major now fearing for Monty's sanity and safety, was loath to leave him alone.

Arriving in Portsmouth that evening, the Brigade-Major went to bed. At one o'clock in the morning the telephone rang. Fearing bad news, he answered it. It was Monty.

'That you, 'Simbo'? I'm afraid I've rather let things slide in the past few days. I want all my papers on my desk at 9 o'clock in the morning, and we'll get down to work.'

Monty had decided to put the tragedy behind him. Grief would be suppressed: only his work, his mission in life remained. The steel of Monty the ruthless, implacable battlefield commander had been tempered. But Fate had further trials for Monty.

Monty mourns. In 1937 Monty's wife Betty died. 'I never left her for the last 24 hours and it was heart-breaking to watch her slowly dying. The final end was very peaceful, just one deep sigh... She knew me up to about one hour before she died, after which she never opened her eyes or spoke.

'I sat in the room at the hospital until they came to screw the lid on the coffin... I tried to bear up at the service and at the graveside. But I could not bear it and I am afraid I broke down utterly... I break into tears whenever I think of her. But I must try to bear up. I have come back alone to this big empty house for good now.'

Removing the Thorn

n the empty Brigadier's house at Portsmouth Monty now attempted to build something from the wreckage of his life. His battalions were ordered to spend the winter studying past campaigns and current German training methods. It was the responsibility of Colonels and Company Majors to teach their junior officers the secrets and lessons of command, as well as how to teach others. 'The junior officer of today is the commanding officer of tomorrow,' he explained. Such junior officers had to be given a chance to exercise senior command on manoeuvres. 'When war comes senior officers may become casualties and this system repays itself ten-fold.'

Monty's 'vision' was not limited to small unit tactics. Though he was still only a Brigadier, Monty urged that a full scale Combined Operation should be mounted, involving the British Navy, the Air Force and the Army. In July 1938, therefore, Monty personally mounted the first and only British combined forces assault landing since the ill-fated Dardanelles. An aircraft carrier, three cruisers and five destroyers made up the invasion armada, with Fleet Air Arm 'bombers' giving air support to a landing by three battalions from Monty's Infantry Brigade, mounted on the beaches of Slapton Sands.

The new head of the British Army, General Lord Gort, came down from the War Office to witness the assault landing. General Wavell, C-in-C Southern Command, watched it from the naval command ship, seasick, but sickened also by the sad lessons of the exercise: 'There was *one* so-called landing craft, an experimental one made many years before...I rather think it sank. For the rest the troops landed in open row-boats as they had done for the last 200 years.'

Monty did not subscribe to the general air of despondency. Weapons and equipment could be easily manufactured. What was more important, Monty felt, was to rehearse the *management* of battle: to dispel the fog of war by a new attention to the human factor. Officers and men must, by fore-thought and by rehearsal, become clear about their roles in modern war. Small scale skirmishes, even battles might be won by new 'gadgets' – tanks, new mobile artillery weapons, dive-bombers. But wars could only be won by those nations which were able to bring to bear the combined weight of their forces: army, navy and air force. Co-operation between the services was therefore a vital necessity. Moreover the *management* of large bodies of men would determine the outcome of a campaign in the field. In contrast to the Great War, modern commanders must make themselves known to their troops. They must command from the front, not from safe dug-outs in the rear. Orders must be given quickly and concisely, communications must be first-class, paperwork minimal. Above all, men must be taught to think ahead. Every exercise, whether indoors on a sand table or outdoors in training areas, must rehearse realistic possible scenarios. Every hour spent in training for future battle would be rewarded ten-fold when war came.

Already, in March 1938, Hitler had dismissed his army chiefs and made himself personal head of the Reichswehr. On 13 March he moved into Austria. Czechoslovakia would be next.

Monty's passionate desire to prepare the British army for modern, continental warfare did not endear him to his superiors. Despite his invasion exercise and a special series of Gas trials conducted in the summer of 1938 for the War Office, he was not offered command of a division in Britain or promotion to Major-General. 'He has some of the defects of the enthusiast,' General Wavell remarked in his report on Monty, 'an occasional impatience and intolerance when things cannot be done as quickly as he would like or when he meets brains less quick and clear than his own.'

Monty's father, Bishop Montgomery. The family fortune had not, however, been made in religion, but in drink. 'I always used to remind him,' recalled Monty's brother Brian, 'that ironically our great great grandfather from whom we were descended in Ireland, was a wine and spirits merchant, and a very successful one. . . There's no doubt about it, my brother didn't really care about being told that too often!'

Hobart in 1902. The thir[...] childhood spent in Ta[...] formative. Though [...] constantly with h[...] freedom and [...] wild, aggress[...]

[...]d a 'colonial', [...]ecome a soldier not [...] his parents wished.

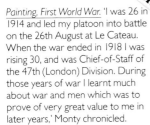

[...]*'s painting of Lough Foyle, Ireland,* [...]*35.* 'They were complete opposites in character,' Monty's stepson recorded, 'but it was an attraction of opposites, and there was no doubt how deeply Monty was in love with my mother.' Monty encouraged her to paint on their travels – in Ireland, Palestine, Egypt and India.

Painting, First World War. 'I was 26 in 1914 and led my platoon into battle on the 26th August at Le Cateau. When the war ended in 1918 I was rising 30, and was Chief-of-Staff of the 47th (London) Division. During those years of war I learnt much about war and men which was to prove of very great value to me in later years,' Monty chronicled.

The lessons were grim. Monty fought in the Retreat from Mons in August 1914, and was severely wounded in the subsequent 'race to the sea'. Between 1916 and 1918 he took part in the battles of the Somme, Arras, Ypres, Passchendaele, the Lys, the Somme again, Chemin-des-Dames as well as the final Allied counter-offensive, which ended in victory.

'The last view of Dunkirk was a blazing town over which hung a dense pall of black smoke,' Monty's artillery commander recorded. 'The sea all around was dotted with life-jackets and masts and funnels of sunken ships.' A quarter of a million British troops were evacuated, but although Churchill told the House of Commons that the British Expeditionary Force must be reconstituted and 'built up under its gallant Commander Lord Gort', the whole army knew that Gort had been a disastrous choice as commander. Monty himself marched into the CIGS's office and said that the events of the past few weeks had proved that certain officers were unfit to be employed again and should be retired. Gort was subsequently removed from army command.

Painting by Norman Wilkinson.

25-pdr Gunners at Alamein, 1942. Monty had insisted that, for the break-in operation, the entire 400 guns of 30 Corps would be under the personal control of the artillery commander. 'The artillery fire has been superb,' Monty wrote to the CIGS during the battle, 'and such a concentrated use of artillery has not been seen before in N. Africa; we could not have done what we have done without the artillery, and that arm has been wonderful.'

Painting by Berry.

The battle of Alamein was the turning point of the Second World War. Monty was knighted and promoted to full General. 'The enemy is completely smashed,' Monty declared to the war correspondents. 'But we must not think that the party is over. We have no intention of letting the army recover. We must keep up the pressure. We intend to hit this chap Rommel for six out of North Africa.' Monty had hoped the Allied landings in Algeria would serve to seize Tripoli from the west, thus severing Rommel's source of supply. But it was not to be.

Painting by Terence Cuneo.

Field-Marshal Erwin Rommel.
Rommel's success in France in 1940 and the desert from 1941 to 1942 rested on the professionalism of his armoured units and his own flair for front-line leadership, but in Monty he was to meet more than his match. Although Monty did not dispose of such professional and highly-trained tank forces, he had rehearsed the command of large bodies of troops in England for two years before his 'call' to the desert.

'We have to be grateful for every day the enemy does not close in on us,' Rommel recorded after ten days of retreat from Alamein. 'I wish I were just a newspaper vendor in Berlin.'

The break-out at Alamein. Monty was disappointed by the performance of the British armoured formations in the battle. He had altered his battle plan when he realized how unprofessional the tank commanders were, but even the modified tasks were beyond them. The Tank Corps was therefore withdrawn from the battle, to be thrown back in behind the New Zealand general Bernard Freyberg.

Though Freyberg's 'Supercharge' attack was successful, the armour failed to follow his example. A final infantry attack on the night of 3 November opened the way, and on 4 November Eighth Army's tank divisions finally broke out into open desert. The battle was won.

Monty in oils, December 1942.
'Headquarters consisted of three large caravans parked close together and covered with a net and bits of coloured rags for camouflage and a few small tents camouflaged in the same way. The portrait was painted in a small tent. . .I stayed with Monty about two weeks,' the War Artist Neville Lewis recorded. 'It was a most interesting experience. As I must confess, I like drinking. A month or so after my visit to Eighth Army Headquarters I was in the Continental Hotel in Cairo when Monty's ADC John Poston walked in: "You should have seen Monty's expression when he got his mess bill after your visit," he said, "He nearly passed out."'

The portrait was sent back in Churchill's aircraft. 'It will be a very good addition to the family heirlooms,' Monty wrote. 'Actually we have none, as everything I possess was destroyed by bombing in Portsmouth.'

Monty in England, May 1943. Coming home from the desert in the Flying Fortress he had won from Eisenhower in a bet, Monty wanted a 10 day rest – but refused to see his relatives. 'I find the various members of my family are apt to be very trying, and particularly my mother – who is on the 80 mark. They are all now writing and saying they must see me if I come home. It will be my one desire to see *none* of them; they would drive me mad between them.'

In London, visiting the War Office, Monty realised he was not only a hero to the men of the Eighth Army, but was as popular as Churchill. Wherever he went crowds gathered and followed him.

Monty's 'holiday' was spent with the guardians of his son David, at Amesbury in Hampshire. 'He looked well but fine-drawn, and he told me he was a little tired,' wrote a colleague. 'No wonder! He was wearing his desert kit, that is to say his battle dress with a sweater sticking out a foot below his jacket, and of course, his usual beret bearing the Tank Corps as well as the General's badge.'

At tea at Buckingham Palace the King remarked on the impropriety of wearing the two badges at once. Monty examined his beret. 'I am told these two badges, when they are seen on the battlefield, are worth two divisions – two divisions!' Monty explained. The matter was never raised again.

Monty at his Tactical Headquarters in Sicily, July 1943. 'The trouble is there is no high up grip on this campaign,' Monty protested. 'It beats me how anyone thinks you can run a campaign in this way, with the three Commanders of the three Services about 600 miles from each other.

'The enemy should never be allowed to get all his equipment out of Sicily, and we should round up the bulk of his fighting troops. . .but such a plan does not exist.'

The D-Day Commanders. Eisenhower, the Supreme Commander (centre), had a British Deputy, Air Marshal Tedder (third from left) and an American Chief of Staff, Lt-General Bedell Smith (far right), serving at his Supreme Headquarters.

Under Eisenhower's overall direction there were three field commanders: Monty commanding the assault armies, Admiral Ramsay (second from left) the naval forces, and Air Marshal Leigh-Mallory (second from right) the air forces. General Bradley (far left) would serve under Monty in the assault phase, but become an equivalent Army Group Commander alongside Monty once two American armies were operating in the field.

The model prepared for Monty's visionary assault landing exercise of 1938, precursor of D-Day, and the only British army exercise of its kind mounted since the Dardanelles in 1915, backed by a battleship, cruisers, an aircraft carrier and a flotilla of destroyers, with 150 light tanks following up. 'An opportunity to practise the very necessary organisation of inter-Service co-operation,' the Navy recorded.

'The invasion was meticulously organised,' recalled a staff- officer. 'I remember asking the Brigadier (Monty) for some amplification of his ideas on this business of inter-Service co-operation – to which I got the simple answer, "Co-operation, my dear chap, no problem there. I tell them what to do and they do it!"'

Monty, at last promoted to General, was sent out to Palestine in 1938 to quell the Arab revolt. Here, wearing trousers rather than riding breeches, he talks to the Chief of the Imperial General Staff, Lord Gort, V.C. 'There is no doubt that we are an amazing people. We never seem to learn from past mistakes. . . The French think we are quite mad as regards our conduct of the war in Palestine. They are expecting trouble themselves in Syria and have everything ready to stamp it out in one day; and they will be quite ruthless; they have 28,000 troops in the country and can cope in any situation.'

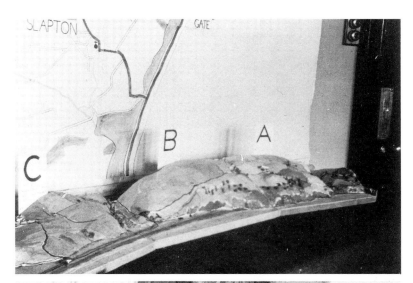

This was the rub. And when it was found that Monty had illegally leased out War Office property in Portsmouth as a fairground that summer (the receipts going into the Brigade family welfare fund), there were calls for Monty's head.

As in 1934, providence now came to Monty's help. The internal situation in Palestine was deteriorating, as the Arabs reacted against ever increasing Jewish immigration. A tough, no-nonsense British commander was required immediately to put down the 'revolt', pending a permanent solution. Palestine, with military bases from which to protect the west's flow of oil from the Middle East, played, like Egypt and Suez, a vital part in Britain's economic and strategic security. Monty had already commanded a battalion in both Palestine and Egypt. To send him to Palestine would be to remove a commander who made the fly-fishing, polo-playing military Establishment feel distinctly uncomfortable. Monty was therefore finally offered temporary promotion to the rank of Major-General in October 1938, four weeks before his 51st birthday and two weeks after Britain and France permitted Hitler to seize the Sudetenland in Czechoslovakia.

To the senior generals of the War Office and the army at home it was exile for Montgomery. But to Monty it was an opportunity to rehearse assumption of command in the field. The new commanding general of the 8th Division arrived in Haifa in November 1938. His territory included Samaria, Galilee and the entire frontier district to the north; General Richard O'Connor commanded the Division in the south. Before giving any orders Monty insisted on making a whirlwind tour of his divisional area. 'I visited every single military garrison, detachment and post in the area; interviewed every civil servant; and talked to every single British policeman. It was an immense task,' Monty wrote to the Deputy Chief of the General Staff at the War Office. 'I got up at 5.00 a.m. each morning and went to bed at midnight. My division is in 35 garrisons and detachments, but it enabled me to take over operational control with a definite and formed policy.'

This was no exaggeration. Within five months the 'revolt' was crushed. 'What has been lacking out here has been any clear cut statement, defining the situation and saying what was to be done about it,' Monty noted – and he had been only too willing to dictate such a policy to the troops under his command. On 15 March 1939, however, Hitler invaded the remainder of Czechoslovakia. Britain and France declined to act, but warned Hitler that if he invaded Poland, it would mean

war. A month later, reporting to the War Office, Monty confirmed that the 'rebellion out here as an organised movement is *smashed*; you can go from one end of Palestine to the other looking for a fight and you can't get one; the Arabs...have had the stuffing knocked right out of them.' The news from Europe, however, made Monty anxious to return to England. 'I have enjoyed the 'war' out here,' he admitted. 'But I feel there is a sterner task awaiting me at home'. He had been promised future command of the famous 3rd (Iron) Division, and he felt its current commander (Maj-General 'Podge' Bernard) to be fat, lazy, and a positive menace to the division's potential

performance in battle. He therefore begged that 'Podge' Bernard be given leave to depart early (he had been appointed the next Governor of Bermuda) so that Monty could take over command of the division forthwith. This would enable him to 'organize and launch the winter [1939] training...I do not want any leave myself. I am very fit and well and thrive on plenty of work.'

Monty was speaking too soon. A week later he fell mysteriously ill, and was hospitalised with suspected tuberculosis. Scarcely able to breathe, he was air-lifted from Haifa to Port Said in June as a stretcher case. His doctor declared that his active military career was over.

Arab prisoners, Palestine, 1939. 'It is an amazing picture. We rope in all rebels and enemies and lock them up; the detention camps then get full; we then have to start letting them out; if I put in 50 I must let out 50...

'However, we seem to win our wars in the end and one must, I suppose, preserve a sense of humour...

'But there is no doubt about one thing. The war out here is the most magnificent training for the army and the RAF and we are producing seasoned fighting men second to none.'

Recollections of the pre-War Years

Lady Michelmore. All three of my elder brothers were different. The first, the eldest one, Harold, was a very keen rider, that's all he thought about. Donald was quiet and studious. Bernard, I don't think he did any special things, but he was a bit wilder, always in trouble. My mother used to beat him.

Bernard was quite naughty, you know, when he was a boy, always in mischief. My mother was very strict, very strict. Bernard used to get a few beatings. We younger ones got the best time, my mother had mellowed a lot by then.

He was always kind to me because I was his little sister, the youngest one. He was very amusing, full of fun. He would write very affectionate letters to my mother, telling her what he was doing in the First World War: 'We're off tomorrow morning, to France and I've just had my sword sharpened!' That made us laugh, even in those days.

He didn't have any girl friends himself, never had a girlfriend.

It was a bolt from the blue when he got married. . .

His wife Betty was a lovely person. I suppose she was plain. She had a very interesting face, not pretty at all. We just took her to our hearts straight away. I remember when she

was over in Ireland with us, I said, "Betty, don't you find it very strange having someone boss you about, when you've always done things yourself?" And she replied: "It's absolute heaven – I haven't got to do a thing! For ten years I've battled to bring up my two boys. Now I've got somebody to do it."

Monty did everything for her. He just opened out, he was so thrilled to have somebody to love. She drew him out to express his affection and enter into family life. For her boys to have a step-father, that was a great thing for her.

He organised everything for her – everything. For instance, when David was born in one of the Staff bungalows at Camberley, I went up to see this new baby. Betty was in bed – they used to stay in bed longer in those days after having a baby – and she said to me: "Oh, Bernard is wonderful! I'm nursing David, and I can never remember which side to feed him from." She'd told Bernard this and he said: "Oh, we'll soon fix that" – you can imagine him saying it in his quick, high voice: "We'll soon fix that!" Now there was a china rabbit on a shelf over the bed. He picked up this rabbit and said: "Now – you're feeding him with the right breast *this* side, so we'll put the rabbit over his head. You'll be feeding him on the left side next time and the rabbit goes over *that* side!" She thought that was great!

Betty's death was terrible. Shattering. The worst thing that could happen to anybody. I've always maintained, that if it hadn't been for Betty's death, he wouldn't have become what he became. I mean, because she died, he flung himself into the Army straight away and became a complete, dedicated soldier. I don't think he would have been the Monty he was, without that. . . He just flung himself into the work, you see. I'm certain of it.

Brian Montgomery It was at Sandhurst that my brother Bernard very nearly got the sack — the first of several occasions. This time it was probably more important than any other occasion, because there's no doubt about it, he was very nearly considered unfit to hold the King's Commission.

What happened was that there was one particular cadet who was very unpopular generally. In fact Bernard always referred to him as a 'dreadful fellow'. So, a gang of equally good comrades invaded his room, just as he was changing for dinner, so he had nothing on but his underpants and a shirt. With a loud shout they crowded round him, and bound him up so he couldn't move. One of the cadets, holding a bayonet, stood in front of him and threatened to destroy him, whilst Bernard went behind him and very unwisely set fire to his shirt tails.

Of course there was a frightful scene. This wretched man had to go to hospital. Afterwards there was a very large enquiry and consideration was given as to whether Gentleman Cadet Montgomery — as cadets were called — should be fit to hold the King's Commission, and if not, to be expelled at once.

My mother heard about this of course, and she was very upset, because at that time my father had just been made Prelate of the Order of St Michael and St George at a big service in St Paul's Cathedral. The whole family would have been disgraced.

So she went to see the Commandant, a Colonel Capper, and she must have been very persuasive, because somehow or other it was agreed my brother should get away with it. But he did lose seniority by 6 months and had to do an extra term at Sandhurst.

To talk to, you wouldn't think her formidable, my mother, but when it came to determination and decision and absolute resolution to do what she thought was fit, she had no equal.

Bernard's regiment went out to the First World War in 1914. He arrived just in time for the battle of Le Cateau, part of the retreat from Mons. His Battalion were breakfasting in a field, when suddenly they were fired upon by the Germans from a ridge several hundred yards away.

So the Commanding Officer immediately galloped up to Bernard and to his Company Commander and said "Throw the enemy off that ridge!" Bernard was rather mystified as to how it was to be done, but anyhow he gathered his platoon and went in front of them waving his sword. However, he'd only gone about six paces when he fell over his scabbard and tripped. What he had not done was to wrap the sword strap round his wrist in the approved fashion. However, when he had picked himself up, found his sword and rushed after his men, he found they were all dead. That was his first experience of battle and, of course, it was rather a traumatic one.

Just after the battle of the Marne, when the British forces were advancing to save the Channel ports from the enemy, they came to a village called Meteren, which was a strong-point occupied by the Germans. The battalion was ordered, with a company of cyclists — which always interests me — and a squadron of cavalry to go forward and capture Meteren.

Bernard was again in the van, waving his sword. They embarked on an advance which culminated in hand-to-hand combat. He told me that he met a large German corporal, so he immediately kicked him in the lower part of the stomach disabling him so that he surrendered.

During the action which went on from the afternoon till the evening, Bernard was shot in the chest. He was fortunate, because a private soldier next to him was shot dead and fell on top of him, and there was no doubt that that saved his life, because the Germans continued to fire at Bernard. When night came the village was finally captured and the stretcher bearers came along to find Bernard, and they thought he was dead. They were about to bury him when he made some movement, so he was saved. Very luckily for him, he went to hospital and recovered, but ever after that he only had one and a half lungs.

In 1926 Bernard was then senior Major in the first battalion of his regiment, and I was a junior Second Lieutenant. He decided that it would be a good thing if a party of four young officers and himself toured the battlefields, particularly of 1914 and the retreat from Mons. We had not got any money. It was not at all a fashionable regiment. So Bernard decided that we should all go on bicycles.

We crossed over from Folkestone to Boulogne and bicycled from there to Le Cateau and the retreat from Mons. We had to follow strict discipline, of course, and move in military formation under his orders and never dismount or mount until he gave us the order. I remember one occasion we had to go by train. We always went Third Class and there was difficulty over taking the bicycles into the carriage. But my brother was quite firm about this and he defeated the French railway official in his usual determined manner by pointing to the Cycling Tourist Club badges which we wore, as being emblems of great superiority and officialdom. This completely bowled over the French railway staff, who gave in entirely.

Then, on another occasion, one wretched chap got very ill. He had sand fly fever and diarrhoea and couldn't really keep up. So Bernard said, "Right, we're going on. Unless you come up and keep up within five minutes, I shall send you home in disgrace." That's the way he treated it! Of course he was right. The fellow did have to pedal on, and he was quite all right. But that was a good example of his determination, and his desire to ensure that young people knew something, got some experience of what war was really like, based on personal knowledge.

Betty Anderson. How did I first meet Monty? It was in Dinard, in Brittany, and my father was home on leave from India, from the Indian Political Service, and decided I should go too, although I was studying music in England.

So we went to a hotel in Dinard, where we spent the winter months. We didn't go out very often, but one night I was asked to join a party and we went down to the Kursal, which is now a casino.

I was dancing very happily, with the pro. I had this black taffeta dress on. I didn't have many dresses in those days, so this felt rather smart, with roses down the side.

I was suddenly called by the party to come up to the balcony, because there was a man who wanted to meet me.

He seized my hand and rushed me back onto the floor. Oh dear, he wasn't a very good dancer and I very nearly tumbled over his feet. He was humming to himself out of tune, 'When you and I were 17'. Well, of course I was seventeen-and-a-half, and I thought to myself, he's rather ancient — and discovered he was double my age!

Anyway, he wouldn't let me go the whole of the rest of the evening, and I had to stick with him. Very determined, he was. And towards the end of the evening he said, "Now we're going to sit out on the stairs."

So we sat out on the stairs, and he began extolling my praises, and saying I had lovely golden hair, and I thought, dear me, it's rather strange all this. So then he said:

"I've made up my mind this evening that I'm going to marry you."

I thought, dear me, I've met a madman. I really did think . . I mean I'd never had anything happen like that before in my life.

So I said: "I'm awfully sorry, but I'm not going to marry anybody. I'm studying music."

"Where are you staying?" he asked — he had a very sort of abrupt way of speaking.

"We're at the Madelaine Hotel."

"I shall be round to see your parents in the morning," he said.

I did all I could not to laugh. I thought I mustn't, because I realised he was serious, but I thought it was most peculiar. I rushed home to my mother, woke her up and said, "Hey, wake up, I've had a proposal from somebody! I think he must be a bit mad — I've only just met him! He's coming to see you in the morning."

The next day he duly arrived, and to my astonishment my mother and father excluded me, taking him into a room to talk to him. I was left outside.

When they came out, my mother said: "This is a very interesting man, a most unusual man, and you've got to go for walks with him every day."

In those days one didn't think of not doing what one's parents told one to do, at least I didn't.

So he arrived very punctually, always on the dot when he said he was going to, and walk we did. Walk and walk. Round the walls of St Malo, across the pine woods, down to the sands at Dinard.

All he talked about was warfare.

He had this little cane he always used to carry with him, and one day he said: "Now, I'll tell you how I'm going

to win the next war. I'm deploying my tanks like this" — and he drew on the sands, quite a big drawing. I mean, I didn't even know what a tank was! Never heard of a tank — nor had many people in those days. He drew this great thing with his little cane, and then said to me: "You know, I'm the youngest Major in the British Army."

I am afraid that didn't interest me. I wasn't the least interested in war. I don't remember him talking about anything else really. He never asked me if I was interested in music or ballet. He never seemed to be worried about what I thought: it was just what *he* was thinking . . .

He couldn't have been nicer. He was a charming chap, but not the sort of person that you fall for when you are 17. I mean if he'd been Clark Gable or somebody — dark, tall or handsome or something – one might have been swayed and have thought it would be rather nice to get married, but I was rather bored to tell the truth. He never discussed books or anything at all. It just seemed to be his whole mind was geared on how he was going to win this war and, I mean, I never thought there'd be a war, I wasn't thinking of wars — I mean, one didn't. I'd been through the 1914 war when I was a child and to me that was the last war we were ever going to see, I hoped.

He was 37 and he'd been wounded badly in the first war, and he'd got rather thin, and he wasn't very tall.

He always used to say to me, "Call me Bernard," but I never called him anything but Monty. He was really rather shy and he didn't show any signs of emotion at all . . .

It seemed to me about a hundred years, but I suppose it was just a few weeks. Eventually I told him: "Quite truthfully, I told you I didn't want to marry you the first night and I don't want to marry you now — I don't want to marry anybody. So let's say goodbye."

"Oh no," he said "you can come to Ireland and meet my mother and drive all her cars!" — quite an inducement as I'd only just learn to drive a car. But I said, "No, thanks awfully, I don't want to do that." So then he said: "Well, I'll take

you to a shop and you can buy something awfully nice for yourself." So he took me to the smartest shop in Dinard, he showed me these diamante bags and things. I said, "Quite honestly, I don't want anything. I'm not giving you anything. I'm really saying goodbye."

So I went back to my mother and said: "Look, I've done what you asked me, but I don't want to marry him and that's finished."

Later, we were going to Switzerland to join a party of friends in the Bernese Oberland. We arrived at this hotel and who should I see, in the lobby but Bernard Montgomery!

I thought, my goodness, here we go again. Very persistent man. He knew what he wanted.

So I thought, what am I going to do?

There was going to be a fancy dress dance, so I said, I know, I'll just play the fool, I'll go as a newspaper boy and call out in cockney all evening — which I did. And Monty appeared as Napoleon!

I said, "Well, do you realise now, I do mean I don't want to marry you?"

And he said, "Yes, I realise now. I shall wash you out of my life. You're the first thing I've not conquered."

So wash me out he did.

He became a very great man. I do feel honoured that he should have asked me to marry him, although I didn't want to do so.

Colonel and Mrs John Carver. Colonel

Carver: The first thing I can remember is, we had a large party in the hotel in Lenk and I remember this little man saying to my mother: "I must come and visit the chateau you've got at Chiswick Mall; I gather the washing and the laundry will be blowing in the wind there."

I thought: what an impudent chap, but I didn't really pay much attention. . .

In the summer following, my mother did show a certain keenness to go back to Lenk. She asked us if we would put our savings into this venture. We weren't quite sure why she was so enthusiastic, because she didn't really play much part in the skiing. We thought it *might* be connected to this strange man that she met there. And of course the next winter when we went back, he was there! I can't remember that there was anything that could be construed as a romantic relationship developing between the two of them. We used to go skiing with him. He was good with boys, he could talk in a way that we liked. 'Let's go here, let's go there, what fun!. . .' We went on these expeditions, skating and so forth. He took part in these activities, was a leader, but not to the extent of being very bossy about it at that stage.

We certainly didn't expect any romance. Monty had a magnificent old Belsize, which was considered a very great car in those days and he volunteered to come to Hindhead where we were staying and take us to Charterhouse. I was at Charterhouse at the time and my brother was about to go, and the idea of the expedition was that I should show my brother round the school.

When we got there Monty and my mother made the excuse that I should go and take my brother around. They then disappeared and about an hour or so later they reappeared, saying, "We're engaged to get married," which knocked us all of a heap, I may say, because being, I suppose, rather insensitive we'd never thought of anything like that!

I think he considered that now he'd become a Lt-Colonel at the Staff College it was a good time to get married. And as we now know, he had made an approach to another, younger lady, that appeared slightly unsuitable, I think even to him. And he then thought that a widow of slightly more his own age might suit him better.

I think he went into it to start with in a fairly cold-blooded manner. But to be quite honest I think he became very much in love and got carried away more than he intended to! I don't think he intended that his wife would be an influence on him – which she was, of course!

I'm sure it was a happy marriage. A lot of people said it couldn't be – you know: 'Your poor mother, what she had to put up with!' But I don't think she ever looked on it in that light, quite honestly. Although she allowed Monty a lot of rope to play with and he may have given the impression that he was the boss and his word went on every occasion, I think she was quite confident that if she really wanted something done, she could persuade Monty to do it.

I think he was a bit daring and he liked taking the mickey. I know there was a picture I saw of his elder brother trying to court a girl and Monty in the background making nasty faces and dropping something on them! I think he was a pest and he had the reputation, when he went to Sandhurst, of being inclined to take the mickey out of other cadets and even being rather brutal to people he didn't like.

Well, I think that continued into later life. I think Monty did feel people didn't love him as he ought to be loved. He did have a thing about his relations – I don't remember him saying anything really very pleasant about any of his relations, except his father, for whom he had the highest regard.

He didn't get on with his mother at that time. Under my mother's influence he did his best to be on friendly terms, but I think he always felt that his mother hadn't appreciated him, and that she had this feeling against him.

Mrs Carver: When Betty was ill in Burnham, I went and looked after David. We played on the beach and went to visit Betty every day. I don't

think anybody was worried about her at the beginning. Matron didn't seem worried. I never saw a doctor.

She was very brave, she didn't complain, and didn't ask for anybody, which made it so sad really.

Monty didn't want anybody to be told – he told me not to get in touch with anybody. As I didn't know the family very well, I couldn't have done. I had no addresses and I didn't think of getting in touch with anybody. . .

She was, towards the end, in great pain and she used to hold my hand and almost crush it. It was very surprising to me that she should be left so alone.

I went to stay with him after Christmas, after Betty's death. It was January and he was all alone. The whole place was organised exactly as he wanted it. He told me all the things that he would have arranged for her if she'd been alive. He showed me her jewelry and asked me to choose some of it because I was engaged to John. He was very nice and very kind to me, in a sad sort of way.

I remember him making me clean his white gloves before he went on church parade. I used a whole bottle of fluid on them. He was very cross and said it was totally unnecessary to use so much of that. But you know, one was used to Monty; I mean, you were always careful to try and do your best for him. I think that was what made him so successful; everybody wanted to do their best for him.

Dunkirk

Monty's sister Winsome was returning to England from Egypt, and travelled on board the same ship from Port Said on 3 July. Monty was carried on board on a stretcher. She witnessed his fight to recover over the subsequent two weeks: 'It was just sheer guts, will power.' The ship's doctor also considered Monty's career over. Monty himself did not. Every day he would be carried up to the deck by his male nurses. There he would get out of his wheel chair and attempt to walk, each day increasing his number of paces.

The ship's doctor could not credit the transformation; nor could the hospital doctor at Millbank, where he arrived, in his own words, 'as fit as a fiddle'. The suspected tuberculosis was revised on his medical records to read an 'infection' of the chest, 'causal organism unknown'.

Far from wanting further time to recuperate, Monty was adamant he should be allowed to take instant command of the 3rd Division, which would form part of the British Expeditionary Force sent to the Continent in the event of war with Germany. Maj-General Bernard was meanwhile taking three months leave, and had gone fishing in Ireland. Monty was not officially due to succeed him until October 1939.

This drove Monty almost to distraction as he sat in his hotel room at Portsmouth, watching one of Britain's four regular divisions at home, untrained and leaderless. Tension in Europe mounted as reports came of German troops massing on the Polish border, especially after Stalin's infamous pact with Hitler on 23 August. At the orders of the Secretary of State for War the British Army part-mobilized, with the 3rd Division *still* without a commander!

Monty, beside himself with anger, rang the War Office to protest — only to be informed that far from his October

command being accelerated, all appointments would be frozen. Maj-General Bernard would be summoned back from Ireland, and Monty's name would go into a pool of unemployed Major-Generals.

Fortunately for Monty – and for the 3rd Division – the new C-in-C Southern Command was an old friend, a fellow instructor at the Staff College, Camberley in the 1920's, General Alan Brooke. Brooke, an artilleryman, had the highest respect for Monty as an infantry commander. Pressure was put on the Colonial Office to request Maj-General Bernard for duty as Governor of Bermuda immediately, and on 28 August 1939, three days before Hitler invaded Poland, Monty was made commanding general of the 3rd (Iron) Division.

Four weeks later, on 29 September, Monty embarked his 10,000 troops, vehicles and equipment at Southampton, bound for Cherbourg. For him, as for millions of his countrymen, the Second World War had begun. Impressed laundry vans had to be used for transport, but this did not worry Monty. It wasn't the equipment that mattered, Monty felt, but the morale and training of the men. At Cherbourg the headquarters staff cars were burgled by French dockers, and from the Maginot Line to the North Sea Monty was distressed by the state of French national morale. It was obvious that if Hitler attacked, the French were not going to fight. The sacrifices made on French soil in the First World War had been too great. Moreover the plans for an Anglo-French advance into Belgium to meet a German invasion of that country seemed almost comical, since Belgium would permit no reconnoitring on her soil or military co-operation with the Allies, clinging to a vain belief that Hitler would respect Belgian neutrality.

Monty did not, however, lose heart. As in the first months of World War I, the Germans, he felt, would initially sweep all before them. But if the Allies withdrew in good order, it would be possible to use Wellington's tactics in the Peninsular War, luring the Germans further from their bases and subjecting Hitler to a long campaign for which he was not economically prepared. Monty therefore set about training his division in the art of fighting retreat: of selecting those obstacles best suited to defence – waterways, communications centres – and rehearsing how to defend them.

His divisional exercises were unique, for in them Monty rehearsed exactly what was to be required of his division only weeks later. For instance, early in March 1940, Monty made his division rehearse a 60-mile night advance. In the middle of the exercise he altered the 'scenario' to a fighting retreat requiring a change of plan: 'our Allies in front had been driven in, our flanks were in danger of being turned, and GHQ ordered a withdrawal to a line on which the Allies would stand and fight.'

Monty's Corps Commander, General Alan Brooke, was deeply impressed by Monty's professionalism. However it was a drop in the ocean. No other divisional commander was organising such exercises, and the overall commander of the British Expeditionary Force – General Lord Gort – was a disaster. A man of great courage, he had won the VC in World War I, but he was of minimal brain and completely out of his depth. Gort's headquarters were worse than those of the BEF commander in 1914, spread over 25 miles (in fear of German air attack) and with a completely unrehearsed plan for advanced Command Posts to be set up, leaving the main Headquarters incapable of issuing decisive orders.

In years to come the Dunkirk disaster would be blamed on French cowardice and German Panzers. But Monty saw that the British, too, had invited disaster by appointing an incompetent C-in-C incapable of running

a modern army. There was nothing magical about Panzers, They were like shock troops, designed to smash a hole in the Allied defences, but incapable of sustaining a long campaign 'in the open'. If the Allies trained hard, kept morale high, had strong commanders and good communications, there was nothing to fear. Instead, as Hitler launched his great offensive in Holland and Belgium on 10 May 1940, the Allies panicked, and their armies collapsed like packs of cards.

At one point in the 'phoney war' Monty had once again come near to dismissal, when Gort's headquarters objected to the issuing, by Monty, of a leaflet on the subject of VD to his troops. Brooke had saved his subordinate, and in turn, Monty now helped save some of the honour of the British Army by the most distinguished display of fighting withdrawal tactics seen in modern times. Moving by night, fighting by day, Monty brought his 3rd 'Iron' Division back to the beaches of La Panne and the harbour mole at Dunkirk almost unscathed. Monty himself became temporary Commander of 3rd Corps at Dunkirk when Churchill ordered General Brooke to return to England. It was at Monty's urging that General Gort, instead of obeying Churchill's instructions to surrender the final British rearguard to the Germans, gave the rearguard command to General Alexander. Monty was certain that the Germans would not risk heavy casualties by an all-out attack on the final Allied bridgehead at Dunkirk. He was right, and Alexander was able to evacuate the last survivors without surrender.

Monty was far from satisfied, however. The catalogue of Allied bungling and cowardice (his own Chief of Staff had been murdered by French deserters) brought him to the very brink of insanity. From Dover he travelled straight to the War Office in London, marching into the office of the Chief of the Imperial General Staff and demanding the head of the BEF Commander, Lord Gort. The BEF, he said, had never been 'commanded' since it was formed. 'For the next encounter we must have a new GHQ and a new C-in-C.'

These were strong words for a Major-General. General Gort's Chief-of-Staff, who had been knighted for his poor performance, was soon writing to caution Monty not to upset the Dunkirk legend of a 'magnificent BEF showing,' and saying that Lord Gort considered Monty had 'come out either a good second or equal first' among the divisional commanders!

This attitude — as if Britain had just lost a cricket match after a great sporting innings — made Monty see red. The lack of realism or urgency, or desire to draw lessons and improve British military performance was epitomised by Lord Gort – who withdrew to an office near Buckingham Palace with his Chief of Staff to concoct his despatches, or account of the British 'innings'.

Meanwhile Monty returned to his 3rd 'Iron' Division as a divisional commander, and with the award of the CBE. He was determined to take the 3rd Division back to France to join the remaining French forces south of the Somme in a new BEF being formed under General Brooke. Indeed, so anxious was Monty to get back into battle that he now refused permission for his troops to see their wives or relatives before re-embarcation for France.

This was a gross miscalculation. As his ADC recalled, the men had just survived an extraordinary evacuation from Dunkirk. They wanted at least a chance 'to *show* themselves to their families' before going back into battle. They booed when he announced his decision.

Monty returned to his headquarters, angry at this reception. But was it his own fault? He himself had always taught the importance of the human factor in war. Men are not robots.

They need to know their commander, respect him and be willing to fight for him. Conversely the commander must know his men, and understand them.

The men of the 3rd 'Iron' Division had trained hard for the campaign, and had fought well. But they were back on home soil, and before re-embarking on another

hazardous campaign they wished to see their loved ones and say goodbye.

Monty summoned his chief administrative officer. A supply problem was 'discovered' which would delay the re-equipping of the division by two days. The division was therefore ordered to take 48 hours leave immediately.

'He got a very high feeling of admiration from the Division for being able to reverse his decision like that,' one officer recalled.

Once again, his men were behind him.

The 'Phoney War', 1939. Monty, commanding the 3rd Infantry Division in the British Expeditionary Force, explains the defence in his sector to the Minister of War, Mr Hore-Belisha, and the Commander-in-Chief of the BEF, General Lord Gort.

Monty had insisted on parading his men to impress Hore Belisha, against Gort's wishes. 'Just like Monty – I will take it out of him for this,' declared Lord Gort – who disliked Monty, and very nearly sacked him when Monty issued a frank warning pamphlet on the dangers of V.D. in his divison. Only the intervention of Monty's Corps Commander, General Brooke (behind Hore-Belisha in picture) saved Monty.

A Name for Annoying People

n fact, Monty's 3rd 'Iron' Division was not called upon to rejoin the Battle of France, for on 13 June 1940 the French Prime Minister told Churchill that France would make a separate peace with Hitler. The following day Paris fell. Churchill wanted the new BEF Commander, General Brooke, to sacrifice the 52nd British Division to 'make the French feel that we were supporting them', but Brooke objected that it was impossible to make a corpse feel. The French commanders had given up the fight. On 16 June 1940 Marshal Petain formed a new government, and the following day requested armistice terms from Hitler. France had toppled.

Would the Germans now invade Britain? Churchill refused to negotiate peace terms with Hitler, but he was not arguing from strength. All military equipment save rifles had been abandoned in France, and plans for meeting a German invasion of Britain were uncoordinated and in the main risible.

Monty's Corps Commander in England was General Auchinleck, who had commanded the ill-fated British troops in Norway. Monty and Auchinleck were soon at loggerheads. Auchinleck believed in spreading his Corps along the beaches, while Monty wished to withdraw his 3rd Division inland in a mobile counterattack role. When Churchill came to lunch with Monty, Monty decided to be frank. It was the first time the two men had ever met, and Churchill, though he disliked Monty's arrogance, was intrigued. New and younger commanders were needed, Monty declared. Anyone unfit or over sixty ought to be instantly removed. As Churchill was 66 this was not the most tactful statement! Yet Monty followed it up by a declaration of his own states of health:
"I don't smoke, I don't drink, and I'm a hundred per cent fit!"

Churchill blew out a cloud of cigar smoke, then sipped his brandy. "I smoke, I drink – and I'm 200% fit!" he countered.

Though Churchill did not warm to Monty's personality ('a little man on the make', he is said to have remarked after the luncheon) he certainly took Monty's military suggestions seriously. The 3rd 'Iron' Division was withdrawn from beach defence and made into a mobile counter-attack division. This policy was then applied at Churchill's request throughout Southern England: 'a division in reserve is worth six divisions on the beaches…'

Monty's superiors resented such 'back-door' pressure. Moreover Monty's new training methods did not find favour amongst those who were indolent or unfit. Promoted to Corps Commander in July 1940, Monty instantly reversed Auchinleck's static beach defence strategy and made even headquarter staffs turn out for weekly five-mile runs. He sacked officers who did not have 'the light of battle' in their eyes, or didn't know their jobs. 'Completely and utterly useless' became legendary epithets when removing 'dead wood'. Auchinleck's time-wasting, wearisome night watches on the Channel coast were scrapped so that the men could be withdrawn from the beaches and trained to fight: training that must be undertaken at every level, from Platoon and Company exercises right up to Corps manoeuvres.

Over the ensuing two years, Monty's training methods were adopted all over Britain. Monty himself, moving from command of 3 Div to 5 Corps to 12 Corps to South-Eastern Army and running vast manoeuvres involving hundreds of thousands of troops, became adept at seizing the reins of a new command, imprinting his personality and expectations on its men within hours. When he took over 12 Corps in May 1941, Monty himself likened his arrival to a 15-inch shell exploding. He ordered the evacuation of all wives from the area and went through the senior officers like an executioner. 'A number of heads are being chopped off — the bag to date is 3 Brigadiers and 6 Commanding Officers,' he boasted to a colleague. 'The standard here was very low.'

Professionalism was at last in, brave amateurs were out.

But still Monty was not given battle command, as disaster upon disaster befell Britain's armies overseas.

Hong Kong, Malaya, Singapore and Burma fell to the Japanese, while in the Mediterranean the British were trounced in Greece and Crete. In North Africa Rommel smashed his way from Tripoli to Benghazi and besieged Tobruk.

In February 1942 Churchill had to appeal for national unity. By June, as Tobruk finally fell to Rommel's Afrika Korps, Churchill faced his first vote of No Confidence in The House of Commons. A new broom was needed, even a new government.

General Alexander, idle, charming and a favourite of Churchill's, was sent out to try to retrieve the situation in Burma, leading only to further disasters as the British retreated to the very borders of India. General Auchinleck was sent out to North Africa to try and retrieve the situation there but by the summer of 1942 Rommel had chased Auchinleck back to

Corps Commander, after Dunkirk. Monty explains the plan of one of his winter exercises to the new G.O.C. Home Forces, General Sir Alan Brooke. 'Monty's professionalism made his superior in Southern Command, General Auchinleck, blanche. 'I used to go and listen in to his lectures – no coughing, no smoking, runs before breakfast – all very inspiring and made me feel a bit inadequate,' he confessed.

Brooke was certain Monty would rise to the top – if he could better his own worst enemy, himself.

the gates of Cairo and Alexandria. In despair Churchill himself travelled out to the desert to assess the situation, and decided to sack Auchinleck. Yet still he did not appoint Montgomery as the new 8th Army commander, preferring a tired, popular veteran of the British disasters in Libya and Egypt, Lt-General Gott. Not even the new CIGS, General Brooke, could persuade Churchill otherwise. It seemed that, however high Monty's reputation stood as a commander at home, he was too unpopular in higher circles to be first choice for a field command. 'You have got a name for annoying people at times with your ways,' Brooke had once written to him, 'and I have found

difficulties in backing you at times against this reputation.'

As the German and Japanese armies swept from victory to victory, it seemed incredible that Monty's reputation for annoying people should have precluded him from being employed in the field. One Member of Parliament even declared that if Rommel was serving in the British army he would still be in the rank of Sergeant, so fusty was the British military hierarchy.

Yet Monty himself remained certain that, one day, his 'call' would come. He was convinced that, if the German army could be brought to all-out battle, he could defeat it by using the

Army Commander in Home Forces, 1942. Promoted to command all troops in South-Eastern England. Monty's gospel gradually spread throughout the land. 'There is no doubt that, however much he was mocked, his methods were copied and in time became the accepted doctrine throughout the Army,' recalled Field-Marshal Sir Gerald Templer.

Monty's imperiousness and his certainty that he would one day be called to achieve greatness, did not endear him to all. 'Of course there's nothing wrong with Monty really. He's just a bit mad,' was a typical staff officer's view of Monty at this time. 'Sometimes one had the feeling that the Army Commander might at any moment lead his army directly across the Channel in a personal campaign to liberate Europe.'

traditional strength of Britain's army, the might of its divisions. In North Africa especially, Auchinleck was sacrificing this traditional British strength by attempting to ape Rommel, breaking up the Eighth Army into small mobile columns or Brigade groups. In England in June 1942 Monty organised an 11-day exercise, both to rehearse the troops of his South East Army in the trials of an all-out, prolonged battle and to demonstrate to senior officers the importance of keeping British divisions intact, 'ready to operate as a complete division'. Such divisions must not be allowed to 'drift aimlessly into battle'. They must be launched according to a co-ordinated plan, kept concentrated,

and given the traditional 'fist' of the British division, its concentrated artillery.

But would Monty ever be given the chance to prove his doctrines on the field of battle? Churchill, in Cairo, now sent orders that General Alexander was to assume overall command of the Middle East, with Lt-General Gott as the new 8th Army Commander. Monty was given Alexander's previous appointment: command of the intended British invasion of Algeria, timed to take place in the late autumn of 1942.

The plan — involving dispersed Allied landings from Morocco to Algiers – seemed to Monty a 'dog's breakfast', with General George S. Patton as his American counterpart. They were due to meet each other and General Dwight D. Eisenhower, the overall allied commander, on the morning of 8 August 1942 in London, when news came in of a tragedy in Egypt. Churchill's chosen commander for the 8th Army, Lt-General Gott, had been shot down and killed while attempting to take a few days' leave. Churchill had favoured the appointment of General 'Jumbo' Wilson (C-in-C in Palestine) to take Gott's place, but was finally persuaded by Brooke to summon Montgomery. Monty was shaving at his Reigate headquarters when the call came.

It was, finally, the chance Monty had dreamed of: to command a British army in the field of battle, and to put into practice the theories and preparation of a lifetime.

A New Broom

Certain writers would later criticize Monty's achievement in North Africa by claiming that he was really only a glorified self-publicist, cocking a snook at the quiet, stoic stature of British generals such as Wavell and Auchinleck in order to hit the headlines. Yet when Monty arrived in the desert in August 1942 he was unknown to the world at large and unknown even to the troops of Eighth Army. He cared nothing for ceremonial drill, inter-regimental snobbery, or publicity. When mounting, in 1938, his great invasion exercise on the Slapton Sands he had written about one of his subordinate colonels — a distinguished officer decorated with the VC:

'He is, of course, a stunt merchant and a very good one. But he is not such a good soldier — firstly because he doesn't know very much about it, and secondly because he is always looking round for stunts which will produce publicity. I am trying to keep his nose right down to soldiering; his Battalion needs it.'

Monty had, in reality, very little time for publicity and stunt-merchandising. It was the scale of the problem which met him in Cairo and in the 8th Army at Alamein that changed his attitude. For by the summer of 1942 the name of Rommel had become better known to the British soldier than that of their own 8th Army Comander — of which there had been four in only nine months. Even German soldiers' tunes, such as Lilli Marlene, were proving more popular than British songs.

British morale was, as Churchill had already found, at a very low ebb. Rommel had been stopped at Alamein in July, but only while building up supplies of ammunition, tanks and reinforcements for a final Axis offensive to seize Alexandria and Cairo. Few people at British Military headquarters in Cairo had any confidence that 8th Army would be able to halt him, and there were proliferating plans for withdrawal to Palestine and up the Nile.

The date was 12 August 1942. At a private interview in Cairo with the outgoing C-in-C, General Auchinleck, Monty was appalled by his apparent defeatism.

He had never liked or respected Auchinleck since their clashes over beach-defence after Dunkirk. If he failed to see the nobility and integrity of Auchinleck's character as a figure-head, Monty possessed a veritable genius for detecting military weakness, whether moral or organisational. His reputation as an uncompromising Inspector-General was considerable in England. 'His appearances weren't visits; they were visitations. A couple of staff cars would erupt into your vision,' one soldier in Home Forces later recalled. 'A tough, stringy, bird-like little man would jump out...Striding on ahead, with his staff stumbling in the sand dunes, he'd make straight for the nearest private soldier. "Who are you? Where do you come from? What are you doing? Do you know what's going on? Are you in the picture? Can you see the coast of France today? Good; that's where the enemy is..." Another officer recorded the 'sympathetic look as if he was sentencing me to immediate execution' when his Brigadier sent him to serve on Monty's staff. 'You'd better be on your toes, or he'll have you back here in no time and then there'll be hell to pay. He'll be up here himself before you know.' 'He spoke as if this was to be avoided at all costs.'

The 'unknown but mysteriously terrifying general' was now in Cairo, interviewing the man he had been ordered to replace at the head of 8th Army. And he was not impressed. Auchinleck was mentally and physically exhausted, having combined the jobs of 8th Army Commander and C-in-C, Middle East, since sacking both his original choices as 8th Army Commanders (Cunningham and Ritchie). Auchinleck had been serving in the Middle East since the summer of 1941; he was a poor picker of men and was surrounded by incompetent Chiefs of Staff. Naturally his pride was dented by Churchill's order for his dismissal, and resentful therefore at the 'new broom' from England. Had Monty possessed the virtues of compassion and magnanimity, he might perhaps have responded differently.

But Monty was not fashioned in that way – either by God, or by his upbringing and struggles in life. The fierce clash of wills with his mother, the sibling rivalry in a large Victorian family, and the tragic end to a brief but happy marriage: all had left their scars on his personality, to the point where many people thought him quite mad.

There are moments, however, in a nation's history when men of noble character are not sufficient. "Mad is he? Then I wish he would bite some of my other generals!" George II is reputed to have said when General Wolfe was disparaged in his presence. Now a new broom was urgently needed in North Africa. Disaster had piled upon disaster, whole nations were being subjected to the genocidal tyranny of Hitler's Nazis, yet still Churchill had failed – for all his strategic genius – to put men in command who would be capable of stemming the German onslaught. The Russians were still reeling back to Stalingrad, no American soldier had yet seen battle in Europe: the broom therefore must be harsh and, if necessary, ruthless. There must be an end to the tip and run tactics, of incoherent command, of unknown commanders, of quarrels between the services and the various arms of the army – artillery, tanks and infantry. The Eighth Army must be made into a new army, with a new spirit and a new commander.

General Sir Claude Auchinleck – the 'Auk' – sacked by Churchill in 1942, after losing the battles of Gazala and Tobruk, and having been forced to retreat to Alamein, only 60 miles from Alexandria. Field-Marshal Lord Harding later considered, 'Although the Auk was a man of great courage and integrity, he had got the Eighth Army into a pretty good muddle and he had lost its confidence. Also I think he was probably tired and exhausted. I was full of admiration for his integrity and courage, but he had spent all his earlier service in the Indian Army and on the North West Frontier. I think that he suffered from the advice of a man called Dorman-Smith, whom I looked upon as his evil genius. The Auk was ill advised by him.

'Churchill was absolutely right in changing over command and bringing Alex and Monty in place of the Auk. It was the change of command bringing Monty onto the battlefield that finally decided the issue at Alamein.'
Monty, photographed beneath the wing of his aircraft on his arrival in Egypt in August 1942. Monty had not in fact been Churchill's first choice. Like so many others, Churchill had a romantic vision of war characterized by mobility and manoeuvre. He had therefore appointed an unknown, exhausted Corps Commander at Alamein to be the new Eighth Army Commander, Lt-General Gott, under Alexander as C-in-C, Cairo.

It was only Gott's death – his transport aircraft was shot down at Alamein – which at last gave Monty the chance he had been waiting for.

No More Belly-aching

Having met General Auchinleck, Monty went to the British headquarters in Cairo. There he summoned one of his ex-Staff College students, Maj-General Harding, to get the 'inside story' on morale, equipment, troops and training. The next morning, on 13 August 1942, Monty travelled by staff car to the front.

At the crossroads outside Alexandria, Monty met the Eighth Army's Chief of Staff, Brigadier Freddie de Guingand, an erstwhile disciple of his from the 1920's. By the time Monty reached El Alamein, he had a clear picture of what was wrong with the Eighth Army and the need for strong medicine.

The situation, in some ways, mirrored that of 10 May 1940, when Chamberlain finally resigned as Prime Minister to make way for Churchill, the 'man of the hour'. Like Churchill, Monty had spent a lifetime preparing for the moment when, on 13 August 1942 – two days before he was officially meant to – Monty assumed command of Eighth Army.

Monty was contemptuous of Auchinleck's erstwhile headquarters in the desert, without tents, located on a dung-heaped camel track, plagued with flies. He immediately ordered de Guingand to find a new site by the sea, dismissed the acting Eighth Army Commander, and sent a cable to Auchinleck saying he had taken immediate command of the army. Then he set off to meet his subordinate commanders and the men who would have to fight the battle.

Eighth Army was in fact a Commonwealth force, comprising Australians, New Zealanders, South Africans, Greeks and Free French as well as British units. To weld these various formations into a new Eighth Army Monty felt he must re-train the men, using the same 'doctrine' he had espoused at home in England: employing the traditional strength of whole divisions fighting according to well-understood plans, with everyone 'in the picture', and with properly marshalled artillery, armour and air support.

Rommel was expected to attack at any moment. A defensive victory would give heart to the British troops, raise morale: and provide the necessary prelude to Monty's ambitious reforms in the army. Monty therefore ordered the entire headquarters staff to assemble at 6 p.m. that evening for a 'pep' talk:

"I want first of all to introduce myself to you," Monty began.

"You do not know me. I do not know you. But we have got to work together; therefore we must understand each other and we must have confidence in each other. I have only been here a few hours. But from what I have seen and heard since I arrived I am prepared to say, here and now, that I have confidence in you. We will then work together as a team; and together we will gain the confidence of this great Army and go forward to final victory in Africa."

This was the start of one of the seminal military speeches in history: quintessential 'Monty', delivered in the open sand by the caravans and operations trucks of Eighth Army headquarters as the evening shadows lengthened and the assembled staff officers listened in astonished silence to this prophet of coming victory:

"I believe that one of the first duties of a commander is to create what I call 'atmosphere', and in that atmosphere his staff, subordinate comanders, and troops will live and work and fight.

I do not like the general atmosphere I find here. It is an atmosphere of doubt, of looking back to select the next place to which to withdraw, of loss of confidence

Churchill visiting Eighth Army, shortly before Rommel's attack. Churchill cabled back to England that he was 'sure we were heading for disaster under the former regime,' and welcomed the 'complete change of atmosphere' in Eighth Army since Monty's arrival. 'The highest alacrity and activity prevails. . . The roads are busy with forward movement of troops, tanks and guns.' 'May the anniversary of Blenheim which marks the opening of the new Command bring to the Commander-in-Chief of the Eighth Army and his troops the fame and fortune they will surely deserve', wrote Churchill in Monty's Visitors' Book.

Monty prepares for his first battle in the desert, August 1942, wearing an Australian bush hat against the fierce sun. 'The new Army commander made himself felt at once,' a New Zealand Brigadier recorded. 'For a long time we had heard little from the Army except grumbles. . . Now we were told that we were going to fight, there was no question of retirement to reserve positions or anywhere else, and to get ahead with our preparations. To make the intention clear our troop-carrying transport was sent a long way back so that we could not run away if we wanted to!'

in our ability to defeat Rommel, of desperate measures by reserves in preparing positions in Cairo and the Delta.

All that must cease.

Let us have a new atmosphere.

The defence of Egypt lies here at Alamein and on the Ruweisat Ridge. What is the use of digging trenches in the Delta? It is quite useless; if we lose this position we lose Egypt; all the fighting troops now in the Delta must come here at once, and will. *Here* we will stand and fight; there will be no further withdrawal. I have ordered that all plans and instructions dealing with further withdrawal are to be burnt, and at once. We will stand and fight *here*.

If we can't stay here alive, then let us stay here dead."

The hush continued. As one officer afterwards put it, "here was a man who had the formula for victory"; another reflected on the "feeling of exhilaration, that here was somebody who was really going to use his staff . . . the feeling that, well, thank God this chap has got a grip . . . He has the meat of the gospel as it were".

Monty's father had been a missionary, evangelical bishop; his grandfather, Dean Farrar, had been one of the greatest preachers in the Anglican church. It was an inheritance Monty had spurned by entering the army; but it was not wasted:

"I want to impress on everyone that the bad times are over. Fresh divisions from the U.K. are now arriving in Egypt, together with ample reinforcements for our present Divisions. We have 300 to 400 Sherman new tanks coming . . . Our mandate from the Prime Minister is to destroy the Axis forces in North Africa; I have seen it, written on half a sheet of notepaper. And it will be done. If anyone here thinks it can't be done, let him go at

once; I don't want any doubters in this party. It can be done, and it will be done: beyond any possibility of doubt.

Now I understand that Rommel is expected to attack at any moment. Excellent. Let him attack.

I would sooner it didn't come for a week, just to give me time to sort things out. If we have two weeks to prepare we will be sitting pretty; Rommel can attack as soon as he likes after this, and I hope he does.

Meanwhile, we ourselves will start to plan a great offensive; it will be the beginning of a campaign which will hit Rommel and his Army for six right out of Africa . . ."

Monty went on to outline his plans for the creation of a 'British Panzer Corps' to be held out of the line, like Rommel's Africa Corps, and used for 'striking blows'. He also declared his intention of stamping out the querying of orders. "I understand there has been a great deal of 'belly-aching' out here. By 'belly-aching' I mean inventing poor reasons for *not* doing what one has been told to do. All that is to stop at once. I will tolerate no belly-aching. If anyone objects to doing what he is told, then he can get out of it; and at once."

The phraseology, the emphasis, the no-nonsense clarity were a revelation to the jaded veterans of defeat as they sat in the sand. Monty was well aware that he would be considered by some to be mad:

"Some of you may wonder if I am mad. I assure you I am quite sane.
I understand there are people who often think I am slightly mad; so often that I now regard it as rather a compliment.

All I have to say is that if I am slightly mad there are a large number of people I could name who are raving lunatics!

What I have done is to get over to you the 'atmosphere' in which we will now work and fight; you must see that atmosphere permeates right down through the Eighth Army to the most junior private soldier. All the soldiers must know what is wanted; when they see it coming to pass there will be a surge of confidence throughout the Army.

The great point to remember is that we are going to finish with this chap Rommel once and for all. It will be quite easy. There is no doubt about it.

He is definitely a nuisance. Therefore we will hit him a crack and finish with him."

'The effect of the address was electric — it was terrific!' Freddie de Guingand, the Chief of Staff, later wrote. 'And we all went to bed that night with new hope in our hearts, and great confidence in the future of our Army.'

Before de Guingand went to bed that night, however, Monty ordered up, against Auchinleck's wishes, a full, infantry division from the Delta, and instructed it to 'dig in' at Alam Halfa, the heights overlooking the southern desert approaches to Cairo and Alexandria. All plans for mobile, Brigade-group fighting were cancelled. A new artillery expert was flown out from England, as well as a new Corps commander to control the British armour, General Horrocks. He was ordered to dig in the remaining British tanks, together with a screen of anti-tank guns, and supported by heavy artillery. Rommel's legendary Panzer mobility would at last be subjected to a drubbing.

When Churchill visited Eighth Army on his way back from Moscow, he could barely credit the transformation. In six days, Monty had wielded his new broom. 'I knew my Monty pretty well by then,' the CIGS, Field-Marshal Brooke, commented later, 'but I must confess I was dumbfounded by the situation facing him, the rapidity with which he had grasped the essentials, the clarity of his plans and, above all, his unbounded self-confidence.' Churchill, in Monty's visitors' book, wrote of 'the fame and fortune' the Eighth Army deserved under its new Commander.

Though impressed by Monty's new 'atmosphere', Churchill nevertheless disliked Monty's plan of static defence. His own romantic imagination and early experiences in the army — including the battle of Omdurman on the upper Nile in 1898 — inclined him to think in terms of cavalry manoeuvre rather than Monty's cold, hard military approach. Churchill admired Rommel, had paid tribute to him in Parliament; indeed, once away from Monty's aura of infectious enthusiasm, Churchill became a prey to doubt and anxiety, even cautioning the British Ambassador's wife to leave Cairo.

He need not have feared, however. Rommel was riding for a fall. He was too contemptuous of British amateurism, and had failed to do proper air or ground reconnaissance. With a German-Italian Panzer Army of almost 70,000 troops and over 500 tanks, Rommel launched on the night of 30 August his much vaunted 'final offensive' on Cairo and Alexandria. The battle of Alam Halfa had begun.

The Downfall of Rommel

Decrypts of German signals (Ultra) had confirmed Rommel's intentions. In fact so confident was Monty about the outcome of the battle that he spent the day of 30 August formulating training instructions for the *next* battle: an Eighth Army offensive to be mounted in October.

At 9.30 p.m. Monty went to bed, a stone's throw from the sea. Shortly after midnight he was woken by Brigadier de Guingand with the news that Rommel's Panzers were on the move. 'Excellent, excellent!' Monty murmured, turning over and going back to sleep.

Rommel was equally confident, writing to his wife that he was 'feeling quite on top of my form.' If he succeeded in his attack 'it might go some way towards deciding the whole course of the war' he wrote, for the Allied convoy bringing new Sherman tanks to Egypt was not expected to arrive until early September. By waiting until the end of August, Rommel had been able to build up his Axis army to its peak size, while Eighth Army depended on a single Brigade of Grant tanks, all that was left after its defeats that year.

Yet when Rommel's Panzer divisions attempted to smash their way beneath a waning moon through the British minefields south of Alamein, they received a rude shock. The minefields were deeper than they expected, artillery shells rained upon them; and the skies above were filled by British aircraft dropping parachute flares, followed by

In September 1942, President Roosevelt's personal emissary, Wendell Willkie, arrived in Egypt to report on the situation in North Africa. 'I recalled the President's warning just before leaving Washington that before I reached Cairo it might be in German hands. . . The British Eighth Army was widely believed to be preparing to evacuate Egypt altogether, retiring to Palestine and southward into the Sudan and Kenya.'

On 4th September Wilkie travelled to Eighth Army headquarters, in the middle of the battle of Alam Halfa. He was taken by Monty to watch Rommel's retreat: and inspect 'the dozens of German tanks scattered over the desert.'

merciless High Explosive bombing. Within hours the Commander of the Afrika Korps was wounded and the Commander of the 15th Panzer Division killed.

For a moment, while Monty slept in his captured Italian caravan, Rommel faltered, disturbed by such bad omens. His theatre Commander-in-Chief, Field-Marshal Kesselring, later considered that Rommel had lost his old nerve, exhausted by his long and brilliant campaign in the desert. But Kesselring was an airman; Rommel, a professional soldier to his fingertips, *sensed* that something was wrong. It was already too late, however. To have retreated would not only have given rise to loss of confidence among his German and Italian troops, but invited dismissal by Hitler, who looked to

Rommel for victory. With some foreboding Rommel therefore ordered his Panzers to continue through the minefields.

Rommel's original intention had been strike as far east as possible, then swing north up to the sea, thus encircling Eighth Army at Alamein, and 'picking off' its units as he had at Gazala in May. However the losses sustained in the British minefields tempered Rommel's ambitions. Instead of encircling Eighth Army, he decided to seize the Alam Halfa heights, the spinal 'key' to the whole Alamein position.

This was what Monty had assumed some two weeks before, when taking premature command of Eighth Army. By immediately bringing up an infantry Division from the Delta to defend Alam

The Battle of Alam Halfa began on 30 August 1942. Decrypts of German signals ('Ultra') had indicated a German attack south of Alamein – ground dominated by the Alam Halfa ridge. But would Rommel by-pass the ridge or attempt to seize it?

'On they come, a most impressive array,'. . .wrote Brigadier Roberts commanding Eighth Army's surviving Grant tanks – nicknamed 'Egypt's Last Hope'. 'I warn all units over the air not to fire until the enemy are within 1000 yards; it can't be long now. . . The battle is on. Once one is in the middle of a battle time is difficult to judge, but it seems only a few minutes before nearly all the tanks of the Grant squadron are on fire. The new German 75-mm is taking a heavy toll. . . The situation is serious. . .'

Eighth Army's anti-tank gunners had held their fire to the last moment. 'When they open up they inflict heavy casualties on the enemy.'

Rommel had walked into a trap, losing over 50 tanks on the first day of battle.

Here Monty confers with Brigadier Roberts and Maj-General Gatehouse before calling off the battle, 6 September 1942.

Halfa and 'digging in' both tanks and anti-tank guns under direct command of his new Corps Commander from England, General Horrocks, Monty seemed to be 'sitting pretty'.

A desert dust storm, however, grounded the RAF. Moreover, when the first Panzer Mark IVs approached the heights of Alam Halfa, they sported new long-barrelled 75 mm guns — instantly engulfing the first squadron of British tanks in flames. Fortunately, however, Monty had insisted on full-scale rehearsals for the battle. The anti-tank gunners held their fire until the Panzers were almost on top of them, and then opened up. As the dust storm died down, RAF bombers appeared, and the heavy artillery massed on the heights of Alam Halfa also joined in.

Rommel's hopes of a quick victory had been thwarted. But still he hoped the British would emerge from their lair and attack the Afrika Korps, which was trained to bring up a screen of anti-tank guns and 88's – the best anti-tank weapons of World War II – to smash piecemeal counter-attacks. With over 200 Panzers still in action, Rommel hoped he might yet counter the reverse he had suffered, and turn it to his own advantage.

Monty's orders were, however, firm: there would be no wild charges or counter-attacks. Rommel would be pounded by air, artillery and dug-in tanks. He would not be given a chance to demonstrate the powers of the Afrika Korps.

'The swine isn't attacking!' Rommel complained to Kesselring when he recognized Eighth Army's tactics. By 1 September Rommel signalled to Berlin that the Axis offensive should be played down in news stories, lest he have to retreat.

Some historians have criticised Monty for not taking further advantage of Rommel's discomfort by launching an attack at the neck of Rommel's armoured

advance and cutting off the Afrika Korps entirely.

Possibly Monty *was* overcautious. This was his first battle with Rommel, and, like a chess player who knows he has a winning advantage, he would not be persuaded to risk it by an unrehearsed attack with inferior tanks. Mercilessly and relentlessly Rommel's forces were bombarded until they retreated to their original lines, leaving almost a quarter of their tanks on the battlefield.

'For the first time since the Germans came into operations in North Africa we were told to do a job we really felt we could do,' one British officer recalled. 'I remember writing home after the battle saying, 'All right, this battle's changed the war. Now we shall win. No two ways about it. We shall win.''

Rommel dolefully accepted his failure, even if, like Monty later at Arnhem he refused to call it a defeat. It was, however, the end of his dreams of seizing Cairo and Alexandria, and thus controlling the entire Mediterranean.

Rommel knew his opponent had been right not to counter-attack. As he later recorded: 'Montgomery . . . would probably have failed if he had . . . There is no doubt that the British Commander's handling of this action had been exactly right . . . for it had enabled him to inflict heavy damage on us in relation to his own losses, and to retain the striking power of his own force.'

In Russia German troops had captured Crimea, crossed the Don, penetrated the suburbs of Stalingrad, and were racing towards the Caucasian oilfields. But in Egypt Rommel pulled back onto the defensive. His attempt at 'final destruction of the enemy' had failed. Attention shifted to the 'final destruction' of Malta. It was Monty's turn now to show whether the British could inflict the first offensive victory of the war on a German army: the battle of Alamein.

Alamein

On 21 September 1942, a fortnight after Alam Halfa, Rommel returned to Germany for a rest, suffering from desert sores and depression. At an interview with Hitler, he was refused further aircraft, tanks and rocket launchers. All he was given was his Field-Marshal's baton, earned at Gazala and Tobruk.

Rommel's hour was over. Meanwhile Monty, 'fit and fresh' in his own words, enjoyed the growing confidence of Eighth Army. On 23 October, Eighth Army would launch its own offensive by smashing a hole in Rommel's northern defences at Alamein, and passing through a British Panzer Corps, backed by powerful artillery. Rommel would be unable to ignore this threat, would have to counter-attack, and in a battle of armoured annihilation, Eighth Army would put an end to tip and run tactics. It would be a 'solid killing match', but it would destroy Rommel's army in Egypt, while British and American troops would land in his rear in North-West Africa.

Leaving only modest forces to man the front line, Monty now set about training the Eighth Army. Every unit and formation must rehearse its battle role. The RAF must play an integral part in the planning, with imaginative deception measures, a feint attack in the South, and a new spirit of confidence from top to bottom.

Becoming nervous at reports of ever deepening German minefields, the acute plight of Malta, and worries over the proposed Allied landings in Moroco and Algeria, Churchill put pressure on Monty to accelerate the offensive, but he refused to compromise. He asked General Alexander to signal Churchill, that if it were launched in September the battle would fail. Mounted in October, he would guarantee victory. Churchill, beset by other problems, gave in.

It was now, however, that Monty came up against a new problem – or rather, an old desert one: the lack of co-operation between infantry and armour in Eighth Army. By training his Panzer divisions to work with mobile infantry, Rommel had created the legendary Afrika Korps, whereas in the Eighth Army infantry and armour remained as separate as the three services.

At first, Monty was disinclined to take seriously reports that his British tank commanders were secretly questioning his plans for the coming battle. Summoning the commanders in question, Monty reiterated his orders. There was to be no 'belly-aching'. The tanks had been given their role and they must do as they were ordered.

But were orders enough?

The Troubles in Ireland had taught Monty that realism is the better part of valour. If the tank commanders went into battle without real conviction, they would fail. Better, then, to alter the plan into one that could not fail. Three weeks before the battle, then, Monty rewrote his orders. The battle of Alamein would not be a tank battle. British tanks would be pushed through the hole blasted by infantry and artillery through Rommel's lines, but would *not* then fight an armoured battle in Rommel's rear. Instead they would halt, and behind their 'shield', the infantry would fight a second battle, eating their way into the flanks of Rommel's front line. *This* would be the threat Rommel could not ignore. He would have to counter-attack and so break himself on the British armoured and artillery shield.

The two main Eighth Army infantry divisions — 51st Highland Division and 9th Australian Division — would bear the greatest burden of the battle, but they were both commanded by strong-willed commanders, with magnificent troops under their command. The Highlanders were anxious to expunge

'*I soon realised that although the Eighth Army was composed of magnificent material it was untrained. . . I was not prepared to launch the troops into an all-out offensive without intensive training.*' Discouraged by the low standard of training in the British tank units, Monty was forced to revise his plan for Alamein. 'The troops in the Middle East had a hard life and few pleasures; they put up with it willingly. All they asked for was success, and I was determined to see that they got it. . .'

Here, troops rehearse an infantry assault.

the memory of their former division's surrender to Rommel after Dunkirk, the Australians were veterans of the first siege of Tobruk. In his diary Monty noted that he had estimated 10,000 casualties in the first week of battle; in his addresses to senior officers he predicted the battle would be a solid 12-day 'killing match' before victory was won.

The battle of Alamein was to be the greatest single battle fought by the Allies in the west before D-Day. No American commander would launch a comparable offensive battle until, early in 1944, General Mark Clark attempted to cross the Rapido and seize Cassino.

Fought in October 1942, the battle of Alamein therfore remains an historic battle, mounted nine weeks after Monty's arrival in Egypt.

Hitherto, Hitler's *Blitzkrieg* tactics had given the German armies a success unparalleled since Napoleonic times, capitalising on shock, mobility, powerful air support, and frightening displays of armour . . . Like ninepins the nations of Europe had crumpled. What Monty recognized in Egypt — as did the new Russian 62nd Army Commander at Stalingrad, General Chuikov — was that these German tactics relied on the demoralisation of the enemy. Once the Germans were locked into wholesale, relentless battle on ground of their opponents' choosing, these tactics would be blunted, allowing the Allies to bring to bear their *own* strengths. Although such confrontations would be attritional and expensive in human life, they would be quite unlike the battles of the First World War, in the sense that they would be decisive, smashing the German soldier's belief in his invincibility in battle, and giving heart to the troops and civilians opposed to the genocidal march of the Third Reich.

In Stalingrad, the defenders proudly proclaimed 'we shall never surrender the city of our birth; every house

of every street is to be transformed into an impregnable fortress'. It was Monty's achievement, in North Africa, to instil in the hearts and minds of his commonwealth troops, serving many thousands of miles from their homes, a similar quality of courage and determination.

'The men were quiet and thoughtful — many were writing letters and you often found the Padres giving a last service to their men,' wrote Sir Oliver Leese the new Infantry Corps Commander Monty had summoned from England for the battle. 'Everywhere there was a feeling of expectation and of high confidence, but a realisation of the magnitude of the task that lay ahead.'

Monty had declared in his 'Personal Message' to be read to every Eighth Army soldier on the eve of the battle of Alamein:

EIGHTH ARMY

Personal Message from the ARMY COMMANDER

1—When I assumed command of the Eighth Army I said that the mandate was to destroy ROMMEL and his Army, and that it would be done as soon as we were ready.

2—We are ready NOW.

The battle which is now about to begin will be one of the decisive battles of history. It will be the turning point of the war. The eyes of the whole world will be on us, watching anxiously which way the battle will swing.

We can give them their answer at once, "It will swing our way."

3—We have first-class equipment; good tanks; good anti-tank guns; plenty of artillery and plenty of ammunition; and we are backed up by the finest air striking force in the world.

All that is necessary is that each one of us, every officer and man, should enter this battle with the determination to see it through — to fight and to kill — and finally, to win.

If we all do this there can be only one result — together we will hit the enemy for "six," right out of North Africa.

4—The sooner we win this battle, which will be the turning point of this war, the sooner we shall all get back home to our families.

5—Therefore, let every officer and man enter the battle with a stout heart, and with the determination to do his duty so long as he has breath in his body.

AND LET NO MAN SURRENDER SO LONG AS HE IS UNWOUNDED AND CAN FIGHT.

Let us all pray that "the Lord mighty in battle" will give us the victory.

B. L. MONTGOMERY,

Lieutenant-General, G.O.C.-in-C., Eighth Army.

MIDDLE EAST FORCES,
    23-10-42.

The Break-Through

Eighth Army's deception manoeuvres had proved successful. German Intelligence did not predict a British attack before November, and Rommel therefore remained on leave. When the guns of Eighth Army opened up on the night of 23 October 1942 the German-Italian Panzerarmee was caught unprepared. By morning Rommel's deputy commander, General Stumme, was dead and the Scottish, South African, Australian and New Zealand infantry had blown the promised hole in the German northern defences. It was time for the British tanks to push through and set up the 'shield' behind which the Highlanders and 'Aussies' would attack the flanks of Rommel's defending infantry.

The tanks, however, would not go through, and Monty faced his first crisis as an Army Commander in battle.

The failure of the British tank units to fight their way out of the gap which the infantry divisions had blasted in Rommel's lines was to Monty an example of the very incompetence and timidity which had characterized British military performance since Norway and Dunkirk. At 2.30 a.m. on the second night of the battle Monty therefore ordered his Armoured Corps Commander, General Lumsden, to come to his operations caravan. Lumsden was told that unless he pushed his tanks out of the minefield corridors and formed the planned shield for Eighth Army's infantry 'dog-fight', he was sacked.

Lumsden *was* sacked a few weeks later, and went to his grave protesting that armour should not be used as a battering ram, but as cavalry, preserving its mobility. In the middle of a critical battle in history, however, this attitude was defeatist. As later in Normandy it would become necessary to use strategic bombers in the 'wrong' role, blasting a hole so that the Americans could be pushed out of the *bocage* – so at Alamein the British tank units

were required to perform a vital, even if technically 'wrong', role in the battle plan. Before the Germans had time to react, the British armour had to break out of the minefield gaps and plant itself beyond Rommel's front-line defences, *forcing* Rommel, who was being urgently summoned from his sick-leave, to react by

attacking Eighth Army tanks and anti-tank guns on ground of Eighth Army's choosing. Meanwhile behind the British tanks, Eighth Army's infantry 'crumbled' Rommel's infantry defenders.

Having threatened to sack Lumsden unless he obeyed his orders, Monty went back to sleep. By the third morning of the battle he hoped there would be sufficient British tanks beyond the minefields to shield the infantry in its next operation: the dog-fight.

To Monty's consternation, however, this assumption proved unfounded, and the second crisis of the battle began. The infantry divisions had

A 25-pdr gun begins the battle of Alamein, 23 October 1942 – the largest artillery barrage since the First World War. One of Monty's first acts, on taking command of Eighth Army, was to dismiss the artillery chief and bring his own young artillery expert out from England, Brigadier Kirkman. Kirkman's brief was to reorganise Eighth Army's artillery in order to concentrate its weight upon the break-in point – 'one of the most important factors.'

'This was essentially an Army battle, fought on an Army plan, and controlled carefully from Army H.Q.', Monty wrote in his diary on the eve of the battle.

Australian infantry advance to keep up Eighth Army's offensive, after the tanks had failed to fulfil their part in the battle- plan. Without the unrelenting courage of the Australian 9th Division, the battle of Alamein might well have ended in failure. 'The Australians established a very difficult salient which they held against continuous Panzer counter-attack. . . They suffered over 5,000 casualties,' the infantry Corps Commander later recalled, 'but they beat off all enemy attacks. They drew on their front most of the Panzer Corps of which they destroyed a great part with their anti-tank guns. It was a magnificent piece of fighting by a great Division, led by an indomitable character, Leslie Morshead.'

Hitler's 'Victory or Death' order only prolonged the agony for Rommel's disintegrating desert army. On 4 November 1942 Monty recorded in his diary: 'The armour went through as the dawn was breaking; it got clear away and out into the open, I and 7 Armoured Divs leading. We had at last passed our armoured formations into the enemy rear areas, and into country clear of minefields, where they could manoeuvre.'

suffered almost 5,000 casualties – the armour barely 450. At first, Monty wished to rest his tired infantrymen and gave orders that Lumsden's armoured Corps *must* smash its way deeper into the German lines. But when Monty's artillery chief reported that Lumsden was touring the battlefield without the presence of or contact with his Corps artillery commander, Monty lost faith in his British armour. 'There is no doubt these [armoured] generals do not understand the co-operation of all arms in battle,' he noted in his diary. 'Lumsden is not a really high class soldier.'

Rommel, however, had finally returned to the battlefield, and the German Panzer regiments were beginning to launch piecemeal counter-attacks, which were easily beaten off by the British anti-tank guns and artillery. An Australian sergeant alone knocked out five German tanks with his 2-pounder anti-tank gun. 'So long as the enemy will attack us, that is

excellent,' Monty noted; 'and especially if his attacks are isolated and piecemeal.'

While Rommel counter-attacked, Monty decided, Eighth Army would *withdraw* its armour, while attacking northwards from the bridgehead towards the sea, eating into the flank of the Axis defenders around the railway line with its magnificent Australian infantry troops. While Rommel's attention was drawn to this threat, the British armour would regroup and prepare for a knock-out blow, through the bridgehead.

When news of the British armoured 'withdrawal' filtered back to London, there was dismay. Anthony Eden, the Foreign Minister, had heard from Cairo that the battle was 'petering out'. Churchill berated Field-Marshal Brooke, claiming that 'for the last three days' Monty had done 'nothing', and 'now he was withdrawing troops from the front. Had we not got a single general who could win a single battle, etc. etc.', Brooke recorded in his diary.

Churchill now feared for his political life. He knew that members of his wartime coalition Cabinet were threatening to resign, and were only holding off the announcement, at Churchill's request, till after the battle.

But his fears were groundless. Rommel, not realizing that Monty had withdrawn his tanks to the rear in disgust at their performance, believed the Australian attack in the north was the beginning of an armoured break-out; and he ordered the entire Afrika Korps into the attack. Casualties on both sides mounted.

Monty watches the climax of the battle of Alamein from the turret of his Grant tank. Because of the constricted space, he was forced to discard his Australian 'sun' hat; and the Eighth Army photographers found the tank beret he had borrowed considerably more photogenic. By pinning his general's badge alongside that of the Royal Tank Corps, the beret became unmistakable to the troops.

Monty's pre-invasion portrait. 'Monty was getting a bit vain, there is no doubt about it,' recalled his Military Assistant. '"Kit – get me the best portrait painter in England", he said. 'Well I went to Augustus John, and he agreed to paint the picture. I explained that the General was not a wealthy man, and John agreed to take a very modest fee.

'"Kit – I don't know where you found that chap," Monty complained of Augustus John. "He's dirty, he drinks – and there are women in the background!"'

The portrait, when finished, displeased Monty and he refused to pay for it.

Churchill pays his first visit to Monty in the field, with the CIGS Sir Alan Brooke, ten days after the D-Day landings. 'If anyone had told me that in four years I should return with Winston,' recorded Brooke in his diary, 'to lunch with Monty commanding a new invasion force, I should have found it hard to believe.' Before lunch Monty gave 'an explanation on the map of his dispositions and plans. All, as usual, wonderfully clear and concise.'

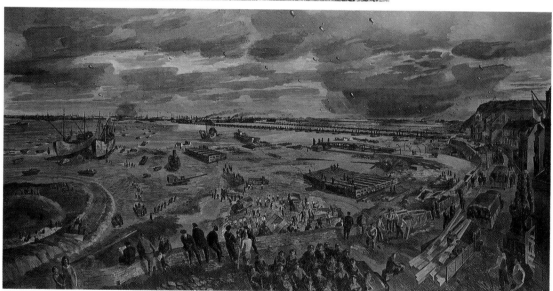

The Mulberry harbour, at Arromanches, Normandy, June 1944. The lesson of the disastrous Dieppe raid in 1942 was that a frontal assault to seize a port would be too costly. By landing supplies through an artifical harbour at Arromanches, the Allies were able to maintain their armies in the field until Cherbourg was captured – and beyond. Painting by Freedman.

Monty and General Bradley (Above).
Monty, Churchill and General Dempsey
(Below).

Monty, Churchill, General Simonds
(Canadian Corps Commander) and
General Dempsey.

Monty decorating a soldier of the 50th
Division.

Monty addressing soldiers of the 50th Division.

Monty being filmed by U.S. cameramen.

Patton, Monty and Monty's Chief of Staff Freddie de Guingand.

Monty painted in the field, at the climax of the battle of Normandy, by James Gunn. Having rejected the portrait by Augustus John, Monty was inordinately proud of Gunn's new picture – 'the best picture he has ever painted; it is definitely superb and will create a sensation at next year's Academy – to which I have agreed it should go,' he boasted.

'The historic march of events continues, and we are now in Brussels and Antwerp. We have reached a vital moment in the war and if we take the right decision we could be in Berlin in 3 weeks and the German war would be over.'

Monty taking coffee, in his mess tent, with his personal staff, 1944: Lt-Col. 'Kit' Dawnay, Major Eddie Prisk (USA), Captain Johnny Henderson, Captain Noel Chavasse and Lt-Col Trumbull Warren (Canada). The painting, also by James Gunn, illustrated the simple, spartan style in which Monty lived and commanded in the field. Together with Gunn's portrait of Monty it was shown at the Royal Academy the following year – where the Queen purchased it, to Monty's chagrin. In a fit of sentimentality he begged the Queen for its return. The Queen agreed that 'Monty should certainly have the picture for winning the war, but for no other reason'. Embarrassed, Monty persuaded Gunn to paint a replica.

'The Queen bought it as an example of a war picture by a living artist, but I have no doubt Monty would find it difficult to believe that she was not really attracted by the subject,' the King's Private Secretary remarked.

James Gunn's second portrait of Monty in the field – this time wearing the badges of a Field-Marshal. 'In recognition of his responsibility for the direction of the campaign in France, which had achieved the decisive defeat of the German armies in Normandy, General Montgomery was on 1st September made a Field-Marshal', his Military Assistant recorded. Patton, however, was beside himself with envy, recording in his diary: 'The Field Marshal thing made us sick, that is Bradley and me'. Patton was determined to race eastwards into Germany via the Saar, and persuaded Bradley to support this axis of attack – fatally splitting the Allied advance after Normandy, much as he had done in Sicily. 'Patton? Patton could ruin your battle in an afternoon!' Monty later commented.

The Bridge Too far: Arnhem, September 1944. 'It is quite clear that the Parachute Troops were dropped too far away from the bridge,' Monty acknowledged after the war. 'If, say, one Brigade had been dropped at the bridge itself, things might have been different. The Parachute people themselves wished it done that way, as they were frightened of ack-ack fire around the bridge itself. I ought not have allowed it. As I was the Commander-in-Chief. . .I must be responsible.'

In fact the British airborne troops held the north end of the bridge for four days with great gallantry before being overwhelmed.

ARNHEM BRIDGE, 5pm, THE SECOND DAY

The King arrives to stay at Monty's Tac Headquarters at Eindhoven in Holland, a few miles from the Rhine, three weeks after Arnhem. Air Marshal Coningham (second from right) had tried to stop the King, having developed an almost paranoid jealousy of Monty since Alamein, and claiming that Monty's Tactical

Headquarters were unsafe. 'This is complete and utter nonsense,' Monty wrote to the King. 'Everyone who comes to see me uses the airfield at Eindhoven, without any fighter escort; no enemy aircraft have been over Eindhoven since I was here. . .motoring on the roads is perfectly safe.'

Monty lectures the King in his map lorry, Eindhoven, 11 October 1944. 'We have all enjoyed the King's visit. He stayed with me as an ordinary soldier guest, with no formality at all; it has been great fun.' Monty arranged for the King to tour the British and Canadian fronts, as well as visiting the neighbouring American headquarters on 2nd Army's flank.

In fact, Monty deplored Eisenhower's conduct of the campaign. As his Chief of Staff put it, Eisenhower's broad-front strategy 'had achieved nothing beyond killing and capturing a lot of Germans and that we were no nearer to knocking out Germany. . .American leadership had been bad, the Generals being too inexperienced. They did not know how to combine artillery with infantry, put all divisions in line and had no supports, so that they were

everywhere too weak. . .'
Six weeks later the Germans exploited American weakness by launching their own winter offensive in the Ardennes.

Monty in his parachute beret, during the battle of the Ardennes, having been asked to 'sort out the mess'. 'I won't add my comment on the war,' he wrote to a colleague. 'There is no ink that I know would stand up to what I would like to say.'

In his anger, Monty summoned Bradley to his headquarters on Christmas Day 1944, and humiliated him: 'I was absolutely frank with Bradley. I said the Germans had given us a real 'bloody nose'; it was useless trying to pretend that we were going to turn this quickly into a great victory; it was a proper defeat, and we had much better admit it, and it would take time to put right.'

Such an attitude, in the hour of American shame, was scarcely calculated to improve Anglo-American relations in the High Command.

On 4 May 1945, on behalf of the new Führer, the German plenipotentiaries surrendered unconditionally to Monty in a tent specially erected for the purpose. 'His lips were firm, and as he finished signing he sighed faintly, sat back and, removing his tortoiseshell rims, relaxed. "That concludes the surrender," he said. The tent flaps were let down, and we walked away over the brown heather,' a war correspondent recorded.
Painting by Terence Cuneo.

Portrait of Monty as C-in-C, 21 Army Group, at the end of the war, by Frank Salisbury. Eisenhower's removal of Monty's 9th U.S. Army under General Simpson had left 21 Army Group with insufficient forces to take Berlin from the West, before the Russians – a decision bitterly opposed by Monty and Churchill. After their humiliation in the Ardennes, however, the Americans were determined that their armies should end the war under an American field commander, and the fate of post-war Germany – and Europe – was sealed.

Monty in Berlin. Appointed British Control Commissioner, and Military Governor of northern Germany, Monty hosted a parade by the Brandenburg Gate and decorated Field-Marshals Zhukov and Rokossovsky, prior to the Potsdam Conference. 'Very hot here in Berlin and we live in shirt sleeves,' he wrote home. 'The atmosphere is amazing. No one knows anything about the problem; the Prime Minister has been electioneering for weeks and has read nothing; Eden has been sick; there is no agreed Agenda. . .'

With the Russians unwilling to govern Germany uniformly through the Control Council in Berlin, each of the four Military Governors was left to run his sector of occupied Germany 'on his own initiative' – 'a hard and thankless task,' as Eden later acknowledged.

Monty shares a joke with Marshal Zhukov, his 'opposite number'. The Russians decorated Monty with the highest Soviet honour, the Order of Victory, and he was fêted throughout Europe as the greatest Allied battlefield general. 'I am now busy getting down to the Government of my 25 million subjects,' he wrote home. 'It is a terrific job and I shall probably go mad before long!'

Patton also found post-war administration a trial, having to read so many documents. He wrote to his wife, 'I am almost nuts.'

Both men were involved in accidents: Monty's light aeroplane crashed on the way to an inspection of Canadian troops, breaking Monty's back; Patton's Cadillac hit a 2½-ton transport truck on a hunting trip. Monty survived; Patton did not.

By the night of 28 October, the fifth night of the battle, Rommel was writing to his wife, 'My last thought is of you. After I am gone, you must bear mourning proudly.' While Monty slept soundly in his caravan, Rommel was 'pacing up and down turning over in my mind the likely course of the battle . . . It seemed doubtful whether we would be able to stand up much longer to attacks of the weight which the British were now making,' as he recorded. The next day he wrote again to his wife: 'I haven't much hope left. At night I lie with my eyes open, unable to sleep for the load that lies on my shoulders.'

He had been a Field-Marshal only four months, and was facing the first great defeat by a German army in the Second World War. Once Monty broke through he would be forced to flee, leaving all his German and Italian infantry and unmotorized troops to be captured.

In fact the German and Italian units fought most stubbornly – a tribute to their courage and faith in Rommel as a Commander. But as the Australian 9th Division smashed its way relentlessly

north, defeat for the Axis army beckoned. 'Rivers of blood were poured out over miserable strips of land which, in normal times, not even the poorest Arab would have bothered his head,' Rommel lamented. Monty's rigorous training before the battle, particularly in night attacks by the infantry, and in the quality of air support and co-operation, astonished Rommel.

Monty, marvelling at the courage of his New Zealand, Highland and Australian infantry, intended now to put his British tank units under command of General Freyberg, the New Zealand infantry commander, who would launch Eighth Army's 'knock-out blow'.

But pressure was mounting from London. Operation 'Torch' – the Allied landings in French North-West Africa – was due to take place on the night of 8 November 1942 – and a clear victory in Egypt was needed if French troops were to be persuaded to change their allegiance from the Vichy Government to the potentially victorious Allies. Monty therefore decided to give Lumsden another

The Commander of the famed Afrika Korps is brought to Monty's Tactical Headquarters caravan to surrender personally. 'He is a very nice chap,' Monty recorded in his diary, impressed by von Thoma's professionalism and chivalry, 'and was quite willing to talk about past events. We discussed the battle in Sept. when Rommel attacked me, and we discussed this present battle. I doubt if many Generals have had the luck to be able to discuss with their opponent the battle that has just been fought.'

'I thought he was very cautious considering his immensely superior strength,' von Thoma later said of Montgomery, 'but he is the only Field-Marshal in this war who won all his battles. In modern mobile warfare, the tactics are not the main thing. The decisive factor is the organisation of one's resources to maintain momentum.'

chance. Instead of putting the British armour under command of his infantry, Monty would let Lumsden launch the break-out as an armoured thrust, aimed at an Italian-held sector of Rommel's front.

Even this attack – Operation 'Supercharge' – was beyond Lumsden's ability. Lumsden had never appreciated the use of infantry working in co-operation with his tank units. In the end General Leese, the infantry Corps Commander, had to smash open a way for

Some of the 32,000 German and Italian prisoners taken during the battle of Alamein. GHQ in Cairo estimated that Rommel lost, in killed, captured or wounded men, some 57,000 casualties, as well as leaving over 450 tanks on the battlefield, and more than a thousand pieces of artillery – the greatest German defeat before Stalingrad, and the turning point of the war in the West.

Pausing only briefly at Agheila and Buerat in December 1942, Rommel retreated across North Africa, relentlessly pursued by Eighth Army. Both Hitler and Mussolini had assumed Rommel would stand for at least six weeks in the more broken country east of Tripoli, but Monty was determined to 'bounce' Rommel out of the port, which would greatly relieve Eighth Army's administrative problems.

It was in the battle for Tripoli that Monty temporarily adopted Rommel's style of command. 'I remember: Monty set off like a forward troop of armour. I mean he had his tanks with him, under his personal command, and they were operating in territory which certainly hadn't been cleared of enemy. It alarmed (his Chief of Staff) Freddie considerably,' Monty's Chief of Operations recalled. 'But I think Monty rather enjoyed it. He was utterly fearless of course – I think he had sterilized that aspect of war completely in his mind.'

Monty's wartime caravans, camouflaged in the desert against air attack. Comprising living accommodation and offices, they enabled Monty to command Eighth Army from the front, with a small Tactical Headquarters unit. 'I told him that things had started well and that Rommel seemed to be attacking piece-meal and that so far we had knocked out 20 tanks with no tank losses to ourselves,' Monty's Corps Commander reported to him at the battle of Medenine. 'He thought for a moment and then said, "The Marshal", as he always called Rommel, "has made a balls of it. I shall write letters." And he did so all day.'

the armour by further costly infantry attacks by night. On 4 November 1942, however, it was all over. The remaining Axis motorized forces were fleeing the battlefield, abandoning their comrades to death or capture. The Commander of the Afrika Korps, General von Thoma, was captured. A weeping Churchill was free to make the announcement of victory he had dreamed of. The Allies had won. The Germans were in helter-skelter retreat. The tide of war had indeed turned.

LOW cartoon. By the time Eighth Army reached Tunisia, its sick rate had fallen to 0.6 per thousand, prompting Monty's senior Tactical Headquarters officer to claim that 'since the advance began Eighth Army must have been the healthiest in the history of warfare.' Over 20,000 prisoners were taken at the battles of Mareth and Wadi Akarit, and Monty's arrogant attitude towards the British First Army in Tunisia and the American 2nd Corps in particular, was reflected throughout his victorious army. 'Monty wasn't the only one that had this vanity: the whole army did! Everybody felt, more and more, this tremendous upsurge, that you were the "chosen", you were the élite, that you were with this guy and he was with you' – Warwick Charlton, editor of Eighth Army's newspaper *Crusader*.
Monty's victorious entry into Sousse, Tunisia, after its capture on 12th April 1943. Patton had failed to exploit Eighth Army's magnificent victory at Wadi Akarit by attacking Rommel's army in the rear, and the campaign disintegrated into a 'partridge drive' in Monty's words, rather than a co-ordinated inter-Allied inter-Army operation.
Tripoli fell to Eighth Army on 23 January 1943. Here, Monty takes the salute by the harbour, as troops of Eighth Army march past in a victory parade, 2 February 1943. Two days later Churchill arrived to review his victorious army. 'I showed him soldiers that I do not believe you would see in any other Army in the world; magnificent fighting men from all over the world; the parade and the march past in the main square of Tripoli was a wonderful sight; the PM was deeply moved and could hardly trust himself to speak,' Monty recorded in a letter home.

"WHAT, ROMMEL STILL NOT ARRIVED? I HOPE NOTHING'S HAPPENED TO THE POOR CHAP"

The Wild West

Like Caesar, Monty could claim to have come, have seen, and have conquered.

Radio bulletins and newspaper headlines soon trumpeted his victory across the world. He had vanquished the legendary Rommel and stepped into history.

The posse of cameramen, broadcasters and war correspondents who collected outside the Army Commander's tent on the morning of 5 November 1942 were astonished, however, by the image which confronted them. Beneath the camouflage awning stood a small, foxy-nosed man speaking in a rasping, high-pitched voice and with complete disregard for uniform. He wore baggy slacks and a grey turtle-necked sweater over his army shirt. During the past weeks in the desert he had tried a succession of hats: a tight-fitting British officer's cap on arrival; then a broad-rimmed Australian bush hat on which he had pinned the badge of every unit he inspected, like seaside souvenirs; and latterly – when touring the battlefield in his Grant tank – a black beret, borrowed from the tank captain. By adding his general's badge to the silvered badge of the Royal Tank Corps on his beret, Monty had found a symbol as distinctive as Nelson's black eye-patch, or Churchill's cigar.

In ten weeks Monty had transformed a baffled, dispirited body of men, far from home, into an invincible desert army. A surge of pride rippled through its ranks, as even the doubters and cynics now swore Monty their allegiance.

Operating from a small advanced headquarters, Monty soon sacked General Lumsden and used his protégé Corps Commanders, Leese and Horrocks. In a remarkable display of modern British generalship he was decisive, crystal-clear in his orders, raising the morale of the Eighth Army to a level which made it invincible by the time it fought its way into Libya. Churchill wept with emotion when he inspected it in Tripoli, in February 1943.

For Monty, the growing fame of his army, celebrated in the film *Desert Victory* (which both Stalin and Roosevelt ordered to be shown in every town and city of Russia and the U.S.A.), was heady wine for a strict teetotaller.

In the field he remained the quintessential battlefield general, leading his men from victory to victory, from Tripoli to Medenin, Mareth, Wadi Akarit, Sfax and Sousse. But when the North African campaign ended in the capture of Tunis in May 1943, Monty flew home to England for a rest. He found himself a star. Crowds gathered outside his hotel, followed him through the streets, brought theatre shows to a standstill – and he gloried in it. Far from being a balm after so many years of struggle, it now gave Monty a heightened sense of righteousness. He already knew he had the loyalty of his troops, who worshipped him; now he knew he had the adulation of the common people at home – wives, sweethearts, relatives of 'his' men who saw in Monty the man who had fashioned victory out of defeat, and now wore the mantle of a military saviour.

He became, increasingly, a thorn in Eisenhower's side. Eisenhower's management of the political scene in French north-west Africa had been

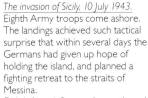

The invasion of Sicily, 10 July 1943. Eighth Army troops come ashore. The landings achieved such tactical surprise that within several days the Germans had given up hope of holding the island, and planned a fighting retreat to the straits of Messina.
Eighth Army infantry advance through an orchard in Sicily, July 1943.

political pressure from above in order to keep their jobs, Monty's loyalty was to his men. Eisenhower's plans to land British and American forces in 'penny-packets' all around the heavily-defended island seemed to Monty the height of irresponsibility. Eisenhower's British air and naval deputies refused to discuss alternatives with Monty. 'A dangerous

remarkably dextrous, but his handling of the military campaign had been near-disastrous, culminating in the American defeat at Kasserine. Beset by administrative, strategic, inter-service and political problems, Eisenhower had left the planning for the Allied invasion of Sicily to amateurs, and Monty, who had already outraged Eisenhower's headquarters by insisting on a Flying Fortress, complete with American crew for the duration of the war, now created further upset by refusing to mount the Sicily landings unless the plans were changed.

Unlike other commanders who were willing to accept bad plans or

deadlock is inevitable', Air Marshal Tedder reported back to London. However, by coincidence Monty met Eisenhower's Chief of Staff in the lavatory at Algiers, and convinced him that if the Allied plans were changed into a single, combined British-American landing, the invasion of Sicily would be a triumph.

Monty's new plan eventually won acceptance, but the weeks of argument introduced a wholly new strain in Monty's career as a battlefield commander. He was as popular with his men and with the British public as Nelson in his heyday, but like Nelson at Copenhagen in 1801, Monty was now, and for the rest of the war forced to serve under a Commander-in-Chief for whom he felt no professional respect. Just as Nelson considered Admiral Sir Hyde Parker to be a worse handicap than the enemy, so Monty deplored Eisenhower's amateur command. Converseley, Monty's own sense of infallibility grew to manic proportions, as he demanded that the American forces for the Sicily venture (Patton's 2nd US Corps) be put under his own Eighth Army command.

Both Patton and the Chief of the U.S. Army, General Marshall, objected. In the end Patton's troops were re-designated 7th US Army, and landed alongside Monty's Eighth Army, but under the overall command of General Alexander.

Alexander also disappointed Monty. He showed no tactical or strategic grip on the Sicilian campaign which began brilliantly on 10 July 1943. The Italians and Germans were caught by surprise, and within four days had accepted eventual defeat. But neither Eisenhower nor Alexander co-ordinated the naval and air force contributions to the campaign, allowing the three headquarters to operate many hundreds of miles apart, in Tunis, Malta and Algiers. The German garrison was ultimately permitted to evacuate the island almost unhindered. Moreover, when Monty found his Eighth Army had brought the main enemy to battle in the plain of Catania and wanted Patton to perform a left hook, as the Eighth Army had so often done in the desert, he found that Patton's forces had flown in the opposite direction to the palaces of

Palermo – with Alexander's weak-willed approval!

Monty was appalled. The bungled campaign in Sicily was, however, only a foretaste of what was to come. Monty

Eighth Army tanks smash their way through a Sicilian village. Monty was proud of the performance of the Canadian 1st Division: 'The Canadians are going great guns; they are very willing to learn and they learn very fast; they will be one of the best Divisions I have in due course.' Bradley's 2nd U.S. Corps was also fighting well in the rugged, difficult

assumed he would subsequently be asked to invade Italy. Even as the battle in Sicily raged, Monty had therefore begun to plan an Allied invasion of the Italian mainland, arranging with Patton in Palermo that the

7th US Army take Messina, while Monty withdrew most of his Eighth Army divisions from the line to prepare for the invasion of Italy proper.

Patton was suspicious. Indeed so paranoid did he become about a possible British double-cross that he whipped his American commanders in what he called a 'horse-race' to beat the British to Messina. When news that Patton had even assaulted American GIs in hospital in his desperation to get to Messina leaked, Eisenhower was forced to relieve him of battlefield command.

Meanwhile Monty's hopes of commanding the invasion of Italy were dashed. Instead of Eighth Army being asked to mount the main Italian landing near Naples, it was relegated to a minor crossing of the Messina Straits, without even a strategic objective – a 'unique incident in the history of war', as Monty sarcastically noted in his diary.

While the veteran Eighth Army landed in the toe of Italy on 3 September, Eisenhower gave the main role in the new campaign to his old West Point colleague, Mark Clark, who had never seen a shot fired in war. Clark was ordered to land his Fifth Army at Salerno – three hundred miles away from Monty's landing at Reggio.

Clark's battle plan filled Monty with foreboding when he heard it. 'You would think we would learn from our mistakes,' he wrote some weeks later, 'but apparently not . . The way the whole party was stage-managed is past belief.'

mountain terrain: 'The Americans have done splendidly on our left and are very easy to work with,' Monty informed the CIGS. But his eyes were on the Italian mainland. 'I would like to take a strong force and sail into the Bay of Naples, land there and capture the city, and cut off all the Germans in the toe of Italy. How about this?'

Italy: A Dog's Breakfast

Monty crossed the Messina Straits on 3 September 1943 with two divisions. All naval craft were then withdrawn for Mark Clark's landings 300 miles further north. This quickly became a fiasco.

Eisenhower and his staff had assumed that the Italian government's secret surrender, signed in Sicily in August, and due to take place on 9 September, would give Mark Clark's Fifth Army a walk-over at Salerno. Indeed so blind did Eisenhower become in his belief that the Italians would turn around and help the Allies fight the Germans, that he removed Mark Clark's American parachute division and gave orders for it to drop 150 miles still further to the north, on Rome!

Eisenhower was living in a fantasy world, ignorant both of Italian unwillingness to fight the Germans and the reality of the battlefield. Far from being a walk-over, the Salerno landings were very nearly pushed back into the sea, Monty's old 10th Corps meeting the brunt of the German attack and sustaining over 3,000 casualties in the first week. The Italians did *not* turn against the Germans, and if the deputy Commander of the 82nd US Airborne Division had not made a clandestine trip to Rome and radioed the real situation, the entire division would have been killed or captured.

What hurt Monty was that the lives of British and American soldiers were being needlessly sacrificed to the ignorance and fantasies of inexperienced Allied generals. Yet even when Mark Clark managed to save his Fifth Army bridgehead from extinction, the Allies shut their eyes to the lessons. Within months a similarly doomed landing would be made near Rome at Anzio. The troops were bottled up on the beaches for almost six months, with over 60,000 casualties,

Turned down for command of the invasion of Naples, Monty was asked merely to cross the Straits of Messina. Monty protested to General Alexander – later referring sarcastically to the matter as 'a unique incident in the history of war': 'I sent a cable to General Alexander saying that I had been ordered to invade the mainland of Europe with the Eighth Army – but had been given no object.'

Monty himself crossed to Italy on 4 September 1943, certain that the landings were a strategic mistake, and that Eighth Army should have been used either to bolster the Naples assault or landed at Taranto. 'I told you I could write a very good book about the whole "Husky" (Sicily invasion) affair,' Monty wrote to a friend. 'It is nothing to the one I could write about the invasion of the mainland of Italy. You would think we would learn by our mistakes, but apparently not... The way the whole party was stage-managed is past all belief' – for within days of his object-less landings in the toe of Italy, Monty was asked to 'rescue' Mark Clark at Salerno.

almost six times those of Alamein.

Such waste of human life saddened Monty. By December his Eighth Army had marched and fought some 700 miles up the east side of Italy, yet Alexander had shown himself incapable of coordinating the operations of the two separate Allied armies. The Allies had failed to reach Rome, and were tied to a winter campaign in the mountains of central Italy, without any strategical purpose other than to 'tie down' German divisions.

In Monty's view Allied operations in the Mediterranean were misconceived and misdirected. Once the Allies were properly established in southern Italy, the 20 German divisions in Italy would be tied down by the very threat of further Allied landings behind their lines.

The Allies now held the initiative. Their air forces were well-established in Italy. As Monty wrote to Field–Marshal Brooke, by holding a strong *defensive* line in Italy the Allies would 'constitute a very serious threat to Germany in several directions: Eastwards into Austria, Northwards into south Germany, and Westwards into southern France. We could play on this and keep the Germans guessing and thus help OVERLORD' – the *real* Allied offensive across the English Channel, set for 1944.

Instead, both Fifth and Eighth Armies were ordered to slog forwards. As in the First World War this campaign was criminal in its disregard for human casualties.

Monty loyally led his troops across the river Sangro, beyond the latitude of Rome, on Italy's Adriatic side, but he remained convinced that Italy was a strategic backwater. The most important task for the Allies now lay in England, preparing the weapon of invasion across the Channel. But would Monty be appointed to command it?

Monty visiting Mark Clark at Salerno, 24 September 1943. Monty had predicted that Clark's landings would run into trouble, but Eisenhower was so pleased with his success in getting the Italians to surrender that he removed Clark's airborne troops and ordered them to land on Rome. Only General Maxwell Taylor's secret radio transmission from Rome saved the Division from certain suicide: and by using it as emergency paratroop reinforcements Clark was able to stave off Allied defeat at Salerno: 'a close-run thing' as Churchill wrote. *'After the Salerno front had been saved, the two armies lined up side by side. We then moved North-West up Italy; there was no co-ordination, no plan, no grip; I did what I liked, Clark did what he liked,' Monty acknowledged with exasperation in his diary.* The Italian campaign disintegrated into a series of expensive battles to seize mountains and river crossings.

Who will Lead OVERLORD?

From all that Monty heard, the planning of OVERLORD, the invasion of France across the English Channel, was in the hands of amateurs. 'Some fresh air seems to be needed,' he wrote to the War Office in November 1943. 'And a good deal of dead wood needs to be cut out, and the whole show made younger, and more virile.'

Monty was himself 56. He went to bed in his captured caravan at 9.30 every evening, making no exceptions. He disliked visitors, and would not even let Churchill visit him in the field:

I have said I cannot have him up here; everyone is far too busy, and my Tac HQ is so far forward it would not be safe for him.

Small wonder then that Churchilll did not favour Monty for command of OVERLORD. In fact Churchill did not favour OVERLORD at all, fearing another Dardanelles fiasco. Only when Stalin insisted upon a Second Front did Roosevelt and Churchill relent. Given the increasing part Americans were playing

Monty had had misgivings about the planning for the Second Front – the cross-Channel invasion of France. 'A large operation is envisaged in 1944. A planning staff in London is dealing with it, or trying to do so; this staff is completely theoretical, there is no one on it who knows the battle end of the problem, war atmosphere is completely lacking. . . The orchestra is playing without a conductor and making very queer noises,' Monty wrote prophetically in August 1943.

Who would command the invasion armies – Monty or Alexander?

Here, the CIGS, General Sir Alan Brooke, visits both Alexander and Monty in Italy on 14 December, before the eventual decision was made.

both in the air and on the ground, however, the supremo had to be an American. General Marshall had always hoped he would be given the post; but in the event, Roosevelt felt he could not dispense with Marshall's talents in Washington. MacArthur was running the war in the Far East. This left only Eisenhower.

From the point of view of the President, Eisenhower had 'done a good job' in the Mediterranean. There was remarkably little friction between Allies at his Algiers headquarters. He was universally liked. He had enlisted the support of the Vichy French in North Africa, and had conducted the surrender negotiations with the Italian government with remarkable skill. The fact that the military campaigns in Tunisia, Sicily and then Italy had often verged on disaster under Eisenhower did not trouble Roosevelt, who had not the remotest knowledge or interest in battlefield reality.

Roosevelt therefore appointed Eisenhower as Supreme Commander of OVERLORD.

Eisenhower now recommended General Alexander as his field deputy to command the ground forces in the invasion. But since the Americans had chosen the overall C–in–C, the decision had to be a British one. Churchill cabled London saying he was considering whether to appoint Alexander or Montgomery. In Italy Monty waited on tenterhooks. A telephone call came through from Alexander's headquarters, asking whether Monty wanted Alexander's accommodation in Naples. Fearing that Alexander had been appointed to OVERLORD, Monty's heart sank.

It was a hoax, however. Churchill had fallen ill with pneumonia. The War Cabinet in London were 'disposed to think that Montgomery would be a better choice than Alexander', given Eisenhower's military deficiencies, and Field-Marshal Brooke was able to persuade the sick Prime Minister to give Monty the job. On Christmas Eve, 1943, Monty received the news.

'When the heart is full it is not easy to speak,' he wrote in his Farewell Message to the men of Eighth Army. 'But I would say this to you: You have made this Army what it is. You have made its name a houshold word all over the world. Therefore you must uphold its good name and its traditions.'

On 31 December 1943 Monty left Italy. He was charged with the greatest Allied undertaking of the war, the D-Day landings.

Preparing for D-Day

I f the trumpet gives forth an uncertain sound, who shall prepare himself for battle?' Such was Monty's favourite dictum as a teacher at the Staff College, Camberly, in the 1920's. In preparing for the invasion of France in 1944 Monty certainly gave forth a clear sound. The decisiveness with troops. Weak-willed commanders were mercilessly sacked. As in the desert before the invasion of Sicily, Monty made it his mission to address every officer and man who would land in France. His theme was the need to get the war over quickly. To do that the Allies were now about to fight the most decisive battle of the war. Tirelessly

Within days of his arrival in England, Monty had recast the invasion of Normandy. Two Allied armies would land, simultaneously, under his command. 'Time is short,' Monty declared to a gathering of Army, Corps and Divisional Commanders at his new headquarters. 'We must stop experimenting and prepare for battle. I will lay down the form; everyone must accept it and act on it; all belly-aching will cease.'

Here, Monty looks out across the English Channel towards the coast of France, during an invasion rehearsal.

which he rejected existing plans of assault and substituted a five-divisional landing on D-Day, flanked by three parachute division drops, transformed a defeatist undertaking (in which neither Churchill nor Brooke had any real faith) into an operation that could not fail. Even Eisenhower, who had originally asked for Alexander to be his invasion field commander, was amazed. He admitted privately, when the war was over, that without Monty the D-Day landings might well have proved a failure.

Monty had made himself master of the set-piece battle. Knowledge that Rommel had been put in charge of the entire 'West Wall' of Fortress Europe only excited Monty's competitiveness. He had defeated Rommel already in the desert; the battle of Normandy would now be Alamein writ large.

Having announced the new plan, Monty set about the final training, rehearsal and enthusing of his Allied

he toured even munitions factories where there were production bottlenecks. He was, in the words of a Governor of the BBC, the second most popular man in Britain.

Churchill was well aware of this. He could not forbear nagging Monty with doubts about the enterprise, and the way it was being mounted. Eventually Monty took Churchill into his study at Portsmouth shortly before embarcation. If the Prime Minister kept questioning the logistics and organisation for D-Day it must mean he had lost confidence in its commander. Did he wish Monty to resign?

Churchill broke down and wept. He was seventy years old, exhausted by his own tireless prosecution of the war, and not in good health.

By contrast, Monty was in the best of spirits, and supremely confident. He would have almost three million British, American and Canadian soldiers under his overall command. His whole life, the long and patient mastering of his profession, as well as the disappointments and tragedies he had had to face, seemed a preparation for this moment. He commissioned the most famous painter in Britain to do his portrait (which he then rejected!), and in his final Message to his officers and men on

Dorset, the invasion armada assembled on the South Coast of England at the beginning of June. Early on 5 June 1944, after one cancellation owing to bad weather, Eisenhower finally gave the go-ahead. And on 6 June 1944 began the greatest seaborne invasion in human history.

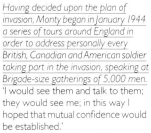

Having decided upon the plan of invasion, Monty began in January 1944 a series of tours around England in order to address personally every British, Canadian and American soldier taking part in the invasion, speaking at Brigade-size gatherings of 5,000 men. 'I would see them and talk to them; they would see me; in this way I hoped that mutual confidence would be established.'

Here, Monty addresses U.S. troops. 'The first one he did with the Americans, he was very nervous. He didn't really know the Americans. 'Now, I don't know you people, but,' he said, 'I know General Eisenhower. Ike and I are good friends and we're going to do this business together. Now,' he said, 'I've never been to the States, but Ike has asked me to come over after the war and I want to go over and visit your country. And,' he said, 'I hear so much about it, and I don't know whether to start in the North or the South.' And some black soldier at the back said: 'What the hell are you trying to do? Start another war?'

Monty's tours before D-Day extended even to factories. 'The war has gone

on long enough,' he declared. 'The women bear the real burden. Let us rally to the task and finish off this war; it can be done; and together, you and I, we will see this thing through – to the end.'

'We shall have to send the soldiers in to this party "seeing red",' Monty declared. 'We must get them completely on their toes; having absolute faith in the plan; and embued with infectious optimism and offensive eagerness. Nothing

must stop them. If we send them into battle in this way – then we shall succeed.'

'Confidence in the high command is absolutely without parallel,' an American divisional commander reported after Monty's inspection of his assault troops, 'and what appealed to them was that the General visited every one of the U.S. outfits before going over.'

the eve of D-Day Monty quoted the Duke of Montrose, soldier poet of the 17th century:

> He either fears his fate too much,
> Or his deserts are small,

> Who dares not put it to the touch
> To win or lose it all.

After two great 'expositions' of the plans mounted at his St Paul's School Headquarters, and a landing rehearsal in

The Battle of Normandy

Backed by a fleet of 600 battleships, cruisers, destroyers and gunships, and supported by over 10,000 fighters and bombers in the air, Monty's armies set sail for Normandy.

History had come full circle, for it was a Montgomery ancestor, Viscomte Montgomerie d'Exmes, who had been William the Conqueror's army commander, later Earl of Arundel and Shrewsbury and a great Norman administrator of occupied England.

Since William the Conqueror, no cross-Channel invasion had prospered. Even Hitler had abandoned preparations for an invasion in 1940, just as Napoleon had been forced to do. To land an army on hostile shores and keep it supplied is the most hazardous of all military operations. Churchill was dubious of success. If before winter the Allies managed to seize only Cherbourg on the North Normandy peninsula, the landings would be 'a wonderfully conducted military campaign'. If the Allies actually liberated Paris by Christmas, he promised, 'I will proclaim that this is the most grandly conceived and best conducted operation known in the history of war.'

Casualties in the assault were lighter than had been feared. In retrospect it seemed inconceivable that two Allied armies could be put ashore with less than 5% casualties when Hitler disposed of some 58 divisions in France and along the Channel seabord. As at Alamein, Rommel had left his command post and was on his way to Germany. Moreover Field-Marshal von Rundstedt discounted early reports of invasion in Normandy, believing them to be a feint.

Monty himself sailed for Normandy on the night of 6 June 1944. In Tunisia, Sicily and Italy he had been hamstrung by being only an army commander, subject to an Army Group Commander incapable of co-ordinating the several armies. In Normandy Monty was at last the sole director of the orchestra, as C-in-C of the Allied invasion armies, and he was determined to make that battle the deciding contest of the war.

As at Alamein, Monty's ambitions were often frustrated by his own subordinate commanders more than by the enemy. The senior American commander, General Bradley, had only ever commanded a Corps in battle before; when the British managed to pull the combined weight of the German armoured forces onto the eastern flank, Bradley refused to comply with Monty's instructions to swing south towards the Loire, insisting that he must first take Cherbourg. This error, as with the British and Canadian failure to seize Caen before the Germans could react, was to cost Monty dear. Channel storms disrupted the supply of men and materiel and sank the American 'floating' harbour off Omaha Beach, giving the Germans time to regroup. Though he held to his original strategy of threatening a break-out in the east while swinging his American forces in a giant wheel to the Loire, Monty's time-table was seriously affected and the world watched with baited breath as the war was slugged out in Normandy.

The battle saw, without doubt, Monty's greatest display of generalship, on a par with Wellington at Waterloo, or Nelson at Trafalgar. Using a team of hand-picked young Liaison Officers and operating from his erstwhile desert caravans, Monty inspired his two million officers and men in Normandy to face up to some of the most ruthless, indoctrinated and professional soldiery in Europe, including Hitler's much-vaunted SS Panzer divisions and to defeat them in battle. A week after D-Day Monty's headquarters had laid plans for an armoured break-out from the less well-defended American front along the Loire valley towards Paris, and, at last, in the final week of July, after trials and tribulations not dissimilar to the break-out

British soldiers come ashore, D-Day, 6 June 1944. Monty's own invasion exercise in 1938, plus the invasions of Sicily and Italy, had given him a unique experience in such landing operations. The scale, surprise and concentration of the assault punctured Rommel's defences with remarkably few casualties.

'No one else could have got us across the Channel and into Normandy,' Eisenhower's Chief-of-Staff confessed privately, after the war. 'I don't know if we could have done it without Monty,' Eisenhower too acknowledged. 'It was his sort of battle. Whatever they say about him, he got us there.'

at Alamein, American bombers were persuaded to blast a hole in the enemy line around St Lo. As the 1st U.S. Army smashed its way through, Monty fed in his 3rd U.S. Army, under General Patton. In contrast to Sicily, Patton had been kept in reserve, ready to exploit a break-through. While the Canadian, British and 1st U.S. Armies held the bulk of the German armies in life or death combat from Caen to Avranches, the way was open for Patton to seize Brittany and simultaneously strike eastwards to Paris, the city Churchill had not hoped to capture before Christmas.

Eisenhower and his staff, still in England, ought to have been preparing for this moment if only because, owing to the growing preponderance of troops arriving direct from the USA, he would soon have to take over command of the Allied army groups in France.

Unfortunately Eisenhower had never commanded troops in battle. He was by training and character a manager, a conciliator, a collector of ideas, not an initiator. As a non-partisan Chairman of the combined Allied efforts to launch the Second Front he had impressed everyone,

American troops disembarking, D-Day. By nightfall, over 156,000 Allied soldiers had been landed. Only on the American 'Omaha' beach were there serious problems, and for a while it looked as if the U.S. 5 Corps would have to go ashore via British beaches. Tenacity and courage eventually paid off, and by mid-afternoon the Americans were moving inland. '5 Corps has made a grand recovery from a difficult situation and I have asked Bradley to congratulate the Corps from me,' Monty signalled.

The break-out in Normandy. By the end of July 1944 Monty's strategy of locking the German armour in combat on the British and Canadian front around Caen, while swinging his American army south through the bocage towards the Loire, had paid off. Patton's 3rd U.S. Army could now be brought into battle.

'I must throw everything into the present battle,' Monty wrote on 1st August. 'The American armies on the right, and the British Army in the centre, are now in the process of carrying out the big wheel that will, I hope, clear Brittany and swing the right flank of the wheel up towards Paris.' Within weeks, Monty's hopes had been realised: the German armies were in helter-skelter retreat, having suffered almost half a million casualties in Normandy.

British infantry fight towards Caen. Monty had hoped to seize Caen on D-Day, Cherbourg after 8 days, St Lo after 10. But stormy weather in the English channel and stubborn German resistance in the bocage of Normandy put paid to such an ambitious timetable. As at Alamein, the battle became a killing match which Hitler could not afford to lose. Day after day Hitler sent further infantry and Panzer forces to Normandy, while the Allies reinforced their bridgehead from England and, once Cherbourg fell, direct from America. It became clear that this was the deciding battle of the war in the West.

Sadly, Eisenhower's impatience at his London headquarters and his failure to understand Monty's battlefield strategy, led to intrigue and conniving in the rear, souring relationships between the Allies.

and his order to commence OVERLORD on 6 June 1944 will always rank as one of the great decisions of the Second World War. But once the invasion had begun, he found himself almost redundant, passing his time reading Westerns, fishing or playing bridge. He answered cables from Washington and telephone calls from Churchill, but he conspicuously failed to plan and rehearse his future role on the Continent. The complete failure of the Allies to exploit their victory in Normandy and end the war in 1944 was his reward. For weeks he had nagged and pestered Monty, calling from London for more territorial gains, more fighting on all fronts, quicker progress. When Monty's grand design for the battle of Normandy finally bore fruit and the German armies seemed surrounded at Falaise in the second week of August 1944, Eisenhower was overjoyed and went to visit the front. 'He is over here in Normandy, which is a very great pity. His ignorance as to how to run a war is absolute and complete; he has all the popular cries, but nothing else,' Monty wrote contemptuously.

This was a harsh verdict on his own Supreme Commander, but Eisenhower's performance as a battlefield general was to bear out all Monty's worst fears. He had not worked out a strategy for the Allied advance once the battle in Normandy was won, and for almost three weeks, from 17 August 1944, when Monty begged him to lay down a future plan of campaign, he dithered and changed his mind, unsure whether to advance northwards into Germany via Belgium and the Ruhr, or eastwards via Metz and the Saar towards Frankfurt.

But, taking official field command

of all the Allied armies in France on 1
September, Eisenhower rejected Monty's
plan for a combined Allied thrust of 44
divisions through Belgium to the Ruhr,
preferring widely separated thrusts from
the North Sea to the Swiss border – as in

World War I. In desperation Monty –
promoted Field Marshal but with only two
British and Canadian armies under his
command – now concocted a plan to seize
the Ruhr on his own: via Arnhem.

The Bridge Too Far

All the Allied field commanders were now bulling ahead on their own fronts, without clear strategy or the resources to ensure the success of any one line of attack.

To Monty this was anathema. The Allies had a magnificent chance to exploit the German catastrophe in Normandy, where the Wehrmacht had suffered almost half-a-million casualties. The allies were frittering away their great victory by trying to do too much at once.

Had Monty been of pliant character, he would have bowed to Eisenhower's naiveté, for the Americans were now contributing almost two-thirds of all troops and equipment for the campaign. But Monty was Monty. He had promised the people at home that, after five years of hostilities, he would finish the war in 1944. When Bradley, now the American Army Group Commander under Eisenhower, declared he did not require airborne troops on his easterly front, Monty requested the whole Allied Airborne Army for his Arnhem operation north of the Ruhr. But it was already too late. The Germans, masters of defence, had been hurriedly repairing their tanks

and regrouping their forces.

Operation 'Market Garden' was finally launched towards Arnhem and the Ruhr on 17 September 1944 using American and British paratroopers to secure the Dutch canal and river crossings ahead of British ground forces. The attack was doomed. Eisenhower had dithered and vacillated for a whole month, and the result, on Monty's and Bradley's and Patton's front, was everywhere the same. The Allied onrush came to a halt. Though 21 Army Group crossed the Lower Rhine at Nijmegen and fought their way to the banks of the Rhine itself near Arnhem, they could get no further. The 1st British Airborne Division which had held the Arnhem bridge for four days and nights was withdrawn, having suffered almost 80% casualties.

Monty was chagrined and blamed Eisenhower. He began an insidious campaign to get Eisenhower removed from field command, even offering to serve under Bradley if it was considered politically impossible to have a Briton commanding the Allied armies.

This campaign was as insubordinate as it was counter-productive. Bradley would not have proved any better than Eisenhower in

Having won the battle of Normandy, Monty felt convinced the Allies must smash their way into Germany on a concentrated front. By seizing the Ruhr, German industrial production could be brought to a standstill, and the war be ended by Christmas 1944.

Eisenhower did not agree. He insisted that, given the growing American preponderance in troops, an American must now command the field armies: and made himself Ground Force Commander as well as Supreme Commander.

In desperation, Monty attempted to seize the Ruhr by himself – via Arnhem. Here he visits a British military hospital in Belgium on the eve of the Arnhem operation, 16 September 1944.

Monty's Arnhem offensive was a disaster: mounted too late and with insufficient resources to guarantee success. Though the American airborne divisions secured crossings at Eindhoven, Grave and Nijmegen, the 1st British Airborne Divison was condemned to a pitiless battle behind the German lines at Arnhem. 'In years to come it will be a great thing for a man to be able to say "I fought at Arnhem",' Monty stated – but the failure of his Ruhr thrust left the British army stuck in a narrow salient, incapable of major offensive operations. Even Brooke, the CIGS, criticised Monty: 'I feel that Monty's strategy for once is at fault. Instead of carrying out the advance on Arnhem he ought to have made certain of Antwerp in the first place.'

over-all command of the Allied armies. Indeed it was Bradley's advice which, in his broad-front advance, Eisenhower was following. Fighting thousands of miles from home and with little tradition of battlefield fighting other than the annihilating 'pushes' of the Civil War, and cavalry manouvres against Red Indians, the Americans were still learning by experience – an experience they wanted under their own American generals.

Monty was dimly aware of this. He genuinely liked Eisenhower and admired Bradley's quiet integrity and cautious professionalism. But war against an enemy as skilled and indoctrinated as the Germans was no game, as Monty knew. The Allies had not the manpower or the indifference to human life that characterized the Russian approach to war. Only by being *more* professional than the Germans could the western Allies hope to defeat Hitler's armies, and the bedraggled survivors of his own ill-fated airborne assault at Arnhem testified to the need for a new tactical strategy if the Allies wished to reach, let alone cross the Rhine.

Eisenhower was not capable of dictating such a strategy. Instead, Monty was ordered to concentrate on clearing the sea approaches to Antwerp, while the offensive against Germany passed to the Americans, fighting on a broad front from Aachen to the Swiss border. As in the Mediterranean it was a recipe not only for failure, but for defeat. Just as the Germans had been able to prepare a stunning armoured riposte against the Americans at Kasserine in February 1943, so now Hitler was able to withdraw virtually two Panzer armies into reserve in the Ardennes, behind his front, and on 16 December 1944 he unleashed them in the greatest American defeat since Pearl Harbour: the Battle of the Bulge.

The epic of Arnhem. 'My briefing from General Browning was that opposition might be a weak brigade group with some tanks – those were his very words, "a few tanks". There was no mention of any armour refitting in that area,' the 1st Airborne Divison's Commander, General Urquhart, later recalled.

'And if I had known? I don't know – at that late stage. . . Everything was in train. The operation had been planned in a hectic way over six days. . . There were no more anti-tank guns, we used every one there was. . . Everyone was so keen to go, irrespective of the consequences, because they were so bored with popping in and out of aircraft, and transit camps. They'd reached the state of mind: "We must go!".'

Of nearly 10,000 men, fewer than 2,000 came back.

The Ardennes

Monty had warned Eisenhower and Bradley that the American winter offensive was a mistake. Time and again he attempted to persuade the Americans to concentrate the bulk of their forces, including Patton's 3rd U.S. Army, north of Luxembourg for a decisive battle for the Ruhr, but it was in vain. Patton was determined to break through the Saar, and Bradley had deliberately moved his American army group headquarters behind him in Luxembourg, rejecting Monty's warning about the thinness of American forces in the Ardennes, the very area through which Hitler had launched his great armoured attack in 1940.

Once again the German assault swept all before it, cutting Bradley's three American armies clean in half, and threatening to roll up the British and Canadian forces in Holland by sweeping through the American rear — exactly as the Germans had done in 1940, when they sliced through the French armies and forced the British to evacuate at Dunkirk.

Bradley did not at first credit what was happening, insisting, like the Germans on D-Day, that it must be a feint or spoiling attack. He continued to play bridge with Eisenhower outside Paris and did not return to his Luxembourg headquarters for 24 vital hours.

Bradley's slow response was fatal. The German break-through severed communications between Bradley and his forces in and north of the Ardennes. Luxembourg itself was threatened, and elements of Bradley's headquarters moved out. In Holland, Monty was soon the only Allied general with a realistic picture of events, gained through his 'gallopers' or Liaison Officers. As the situation deteriorated, logic dictated that Monty should be given command of all the American forces cut off by the German attack, the 9th and 1st U.S. Armies. Yet to do this would be tacit surrender to Monty's three-month campaign to get Eisenhower's hand 'removed from the tiller' of Allied operations in the field. Only when Intelligence indicated that the Germans were in greater strength than ever believed possible, and after five days of confusion and dithering, did Eisenhower finally hand over command in the north to Monty.

This was Monty's hour. Since his relegation to command of the British and Canadian armies on 1 September and the failure of Arnhem, Monty had been like a king without a crown. He was contemptuous of the American approach to war but was denied the men and weapons under his own command to demonstrate, as at Alamein and in Normandy, how to fight and defeat the Germans. Now suddenly he was restored to command of four Allied armies in the field, with more than two million troops. He called for his Rolls Royce, a Union Jack pennant and police outriders. Then he set off for the headquarters of 1st U.S. Army 'like Christ come to cleanse the Temple'. He ordered the instant creation of an American reserve Corps under General 'Lightning Joe' Collins (a veteran of Normandy), reorganised the American defensive line in the Ardennes, and echeloned behind it a reserve British Corps just in case the Germans did succeed in crossing the Meuse.

The speed, decisiveness and clarity with which Monty took charge of the battle astonished the Americans — and the Germans. In Normandy Monty had fought the decisive offensive battle in the west; in the Ardennes, in December 1944, Monty fought the decisive defensive battle. Meanwhile both Eisenhower and Bradley cowered in their headquarters at Paris and Luxembourg, so fearful of German assassination squads that Eisenhower slept in his office, and Bradley even stripped off his badges of rank.

It was now, however, that Monty's

prickly, self-righteous and overweening arrogance betrayed him. He summoned Bradley to a meeting at his Dutch headquarters on Christmas Day, humiliating him by making him 'own up' to his mistakes throughout the autumn. Then he sent a message to Eisenhower, refusing to counter-attack in the Ardennes and demanding sole charge of the next Allied offensive into Germany, which would be mounted further north, towards the Ruhr.

Shamed by the American débâcle in the Ardennes, Eisenhower had had enough. He drafted a cable to his boss in Washington, General Marshall, saying he could no longer serve with Monty. The Combined Chiefs of Staff must choose between them.

The Battle of the Bulge. Monty's warnings that the American troops in the Ardennes were vulnerable to German counter-attack fell on deaf ears. On 16 December 1944 Hitler sent three German armies through the Ardennes in a blitz offensive that split the American armies apart. Bradley, in Luxembourg, lost contact with his two northern army commanders, and fatally underestimated the scale of the German attack. When news came of German assassination squads, both Eisenhower and Bradley locked themselves away in their headquarters – Bradley even hiding his conspicuous new Cadillac and stripping off his badges of rank lest he be recognised.

Finally, on 20 December 1944, Monty was asked to take command of the battle of the Ardennes. 'The Americans have taken the most awful "bloody nose" and been cut clean in half. I now once more find myself commander of two American armies, as well as 21 Army Group, and am trying to clear up the mess,' Monty wrote to a colleague.

Here Monty poses with his British, American and Canadian generals (Dempsey, Hodges, Simpson and Crerar).

American infantry in the Ardennes. As soon as he received Eisenhower's telephone call asking him to take over in the Ardennes, Monty set about re-organizing the American front, creating a reserve American Corps under 'Lightning Joe' Collins, backed by a further British Corps of four divisions behind the Meuse. Within two days Monty was reporting to the War Office that he had 'tidied up the mess and have got the two American armies properly organised.'

'I shall always feel that Rundstedt was beaten by the good fighting qualities of the American soldier and by the team-work of the Allies,' Monty announced as the Germans began to withdraw, but by then the *amour-propre* of Bradley and his staff had been indelibly damaged by the U.S. humiliation in the Ardennes.

In bitter winter conditions, Patton's 3rd U.S. Army attempted to relieve Bastogne and 'finish the Germans completely,' from the south. Monty was contemptuous, feeling that Bradley and Patton were fighting in the southern Ardennes for the sake of fighting, with no strategic purpose whatsoever. 'The Germans are in great strength,' Monty pointed out. 'The American divisions are either weak or inexperienced and there has been a tendency in the south to throw them in piecemeal and on wide fronts as they become available.' After three further weeks of unnecessary and futile American casualties in the Ardennes, Monty stated tartly: 'so far as I can see the Ardennes battle is being continued for the sole reason of keeping Bradley employed offensively.'

Humble Pie

Monty's approach to war was simple — a simplicity which allowed no shades of meaning. As such, it gave heart to men who were discouraged or confused. Monty's infectious self-confidence, his ability to reduce the most complex operations of war to fundamental principles, his willingness to delegate responsibility, bring on younger commanders and weed out 'dead wood' were qualities that raised him head and shoulders above any other Allied fighting general: when properly harnessed. Field Marshal von Rundstedt once remarked that generals were like race horses. They were supposed to win. He knew the Americans didn't like Montgomery, but Montgomery won his battles.

For the Germans, this was enough. Coalition warfare demands, however, other qualities and Monty's blinkered professionalism as a soldier was his undoing as a coalition general. The Americans simply did not have an Army Group Commander of Monty's calibre,

but they were damned if at this final stage of the war they were going to accept a Briton, except *in extremis*. In the Ardennes Eisenhower had imposed a news black-out and depended on Monty to restore order out of chaos. Now that the German offensive had been halted, however, he changed his tune. General Marshall had sent a message from Washington that Eisenhower was not, under *any* circumstances, to bow to British pressure for Monty to become Eisenhower's field deputy, fighting his battles for him. By showing Monty's Chief of Staff this cable, as well as hinting that Alexander might be brought from Italy to replace Monty, the Americans forced Monty to eat his words.

Monty humbly apologized and asked Eisenhower to tear up his rude demand for permanent command of the Allied armies. Monty's rift with Eisenhower was, however, symptomatic of a growing rift between the Allies. When Monty gave a Press Conference on 6 January 1945 to appeal for unity, the Press in Britain and America seized on his misguided remarks, and an inter-Allied crisis loomed. An infuriated Bradley

As the Allies neared the Rhine and the end of the war loomed, Monty's fame grew and grew. 'In my opinion, the campaign to set up Monty and, in general, to increase British prestige in this campaign, out of all proportion to the effort they have in it, is definitely harmful to relations between the British and ourselves,' Bradley protested. 'Our own (American) interests should come first.'

After much argument, Monty's strategy for enveloping the Ruhr was finally adopted, with Monty being given the major offensive role in the north and retaining one American army, as well as his British and Canadian armies. Bradley was furious – and determined to pay Monty out before the war's end.

demanded his two American armies back, forcing Eisenhower to act more and more as peace-maker between his own warring commanders.

Whether this could have been avoided is debatable. By now the Americans were contributing more than three-quarters of the troops and equipment for the campaign against Germany. Naturally they wanted this to be reflected in the command arrangements in North-West Europe. With a Briton commanding two of Bradley's three American armies and refusing to mount costly counter-attacks in the Ardennes — which in Monty's view would lead nowhere – they longed to see the back of him.

Monty, by contrast, knew that there was much hard fighting ahead before the war was won. The Allies had still not reached the Ruhr, the Saar, or the Rhine. If Monty enjoyed almost Nelsonian popularity among his men, it was because the men respected his unique professionalism. They knew that he fought according to basic principles of war, one of which was a genuine concern

for casualties. So, while Americans were fearful of Monty stealing their glory, his own troops worshipped him as a general who would only put them into battle according to a well-considered tactical plan, with a proper chance of success.

When Monty squeezed the Germans out of the 'bulge' in the Ardennes, Eisenhower deliberately removed 1st U.S. Army from Monty's command and gave it back to a grateful Bradley, who urged that the fighting should continue in the Ardennes as the main Allied offensive. In Monty's eyes this was criminal. A campaign was being conducted in appalling weather, in miserable terrain, 'for the sole purpose of keeping Bradley employed'.

Eventually, in February 1945, Eisenhower was forced to close down Bradley's front. Monty was at last given sufficient American troops to stage a properly planned pincer attack to reach the Rhine north of the Ruhr. Bradley was furious. He vowed he would one day have his revenge. Eight weeks later he did, by refusing to let Monty's American troops seize Berlin.

Churchill is driven in Monty's jeep to witness the climax of the war in the West: the crossing of the Rhine. 'I didn't want him but he was determined to come; so I have invited him to keep the peace,' Monty wrote. Even Brooke, the CIGS, could not stop Churchill. 'He will be difficult to manage and has no business to be going. All he will do is to endanger life unnecessarily. However, nothing on earth will stop him.'

The Lüneburg Surrender

The success of Monty's pincer attack in the Rhineland, beginning on 8 February 1945, caused a domino effect which then rippled southwards as the Germans gave up their attempt to fight west of the Rhine. Yet the Rhine itself was no barrier. By 7 March 1945 American forces seized the Remagen bridge; and two weeks later Monty crossed the river with two Allied armies on a 20-mile front, preceded by massive parachute drops.

Days later the Ruhr would be surrounded, and with the Russians still stalled on the Oder, east of Berlin, the Allies would have a second chance to seize the German capital. Monty's plan was to race to the Elbe and Berlin, while the Canadian army sealed off the North Sea ports: 'I have ordered 9th and 2nd Armies to move their armoured and mobile forces forward at once, and to get through to the Elbe with the utmost speed and drive,' Monty cabled Eisenhower, adding his own route of advance: 'Munster — Hannover thence via the Autobahn to Berlin I hope.'

It was 27 March 1945, only four days after the crossing of the Rhine. German resistance in the west had collapsed, but Eisenhower, completely out of touch with battlefield reality at his headquarters east of Paris, now cast away the greatest opportunity of his military life. Without reference to Churchill, let alone Monty, Eisenhower cabled Stalin to say the Allies would concentrate on mopping up the Ruhr, but would not take Berlin, preferring to meet the Russians in Dresden! As Dresden was as much in the area designated for Soviet Occupation after the war as Berlin, Eisenhower's unilateral decision came as an incomprehensible blow to the British.

Monty was ordered to give back his American 9th Army to Bradley, and to consider his front secondary to the 'main' American operations further south.

In Monty's eyes, this was Eisenhower's worst mistake of the war. It was the day the Allies cast away their final, triumphant victory. Instead of exploiting the German collapse, Eisenhower spent weeks 'mopping up' a surrounded Ruhr (already blitzed by bombing attacks) and crediting rumours of a last German 'redoubt' in the mountains of Bavaria. Behind Eisenhower's incompetence Monty detected the hand of General Bradley out for vengeance. Bradley had lunched with Eisenhower on the day Eisenhower closed down Monty's thrust to Berlin and cabled Stalin; the Ruhr was part of Bradley's front and Dresden was due west of Bradley's headquarters.

Even Patton was dismayed by Bradley's and Eisenhower's mistake. Bradley was too naive to see the political consequences of failing to seize Berlin and Prague while within their grasp, and Eisenhower was too anxious to make up to Bradley for the American humiliation in the Ardennes.

Monty's chagrin would last the rest of his life. It was a disappointment made all the more galling when one of his personal Liaison Officers, who had served him since Alamein, was ambushed on his way back from a mission to the front near Lüneburg. Aged 25, John Poston was bayonetted to death after he had surrendered. Monty, tears in his eyes, ordered his doctor to go to the Lüneburg Forest, find the body and bring it back to Tac Headquarters for a proper burial, with full military honours. A grave was dug a stone's throw from Monty's caravan. As the bugler sounded the Last Post, Monty wept openly. Poston's death ended the romance of Monty's great march from Alamein across North Africa, Sicily, Italy, France, Belgium, Holland and across the Rhine towards the Elbe and Berlin.

Several days later Hitler's successor as *Reichsführer*, Grand Admiral Doenitz, sent emissaries to Lüneburg to sue for

Monty visits one of his British Army crossings over the Rhine, with General Dempsey and the Prime Minister. 'A bounder, a complete egoist,' one of Monty's new Liaison Officers noted in his diary; 'a very kind man, very thoughtful to his subordinates, a lucid tactician, a great commander.'

Monty was elated by his success in crossing the Rhine: 'We have got six divisions over the Rhine, including two airborne,' he signalled on the first night of operations. The next objective, in his eyes, was Berlin.

Monty's thrust to Berlin was halted by Eisenhower – who took away Monty's 9th U.S. Army and restored it to Bradley: with orders merely to mop up the Ruhr, leaving the Russians to take Berlin from the east. 'I consider we are about to make a terrible mistake,' Monty protested, but in vain. To add to his despair at the higher conduct of the war, Monty's favourite Liaison Officer was now ambushed on a mission to the front line and killed. Monty, distraught, had his body dug up and re-buried, with full military honours, a stone's throw from his caravan at Soltau.

Following the death of John Poston, Monty locked himself away in his caravan for several days, refusing to see anyone. But on 2 May 1945 his troops crossed the Elbe and beat the Russians to Lübeck, thus sealing off the Danish peninsula. The following day emissaries arrived from Hitler's successor, Admiral Doenitz, to sue for peace.

Monty gave the delegation 24 hours to surrender all German forces in northern Europe, unconditionally. 'If they refused to agree, then I would go on fighting and a great many soldiers and civilians would be killed.'

surrender.

Monty lined them up outside his caravans on Lüneburg Heath and made them stand there, saluting the Union Jack. Within 24 hours they surrendered all forces in northern Germany, Holland and Denmark. Before BBC microphones linked to London and the rest of the world, Monty called on each of the German delegation to sign, or he would order hostilities to reopen.

The Germans signed. For Monty and the troops of the British Commonwealth the war in the west was over.

It was 6.30 p.m. on 4 May 1945, almost five years since Hitler's attack on Western Europe. In that time Monty had been personally responsible for the renascence of British arms. From the time of the defeat of the BEF at Dunkirk he had concentrated on re-training the British Army at home, then led its armies in the greatest march of victories in British military history. Jealous minds still abhorred his bumptious ego and his blinkered approach, preferring nice men like Alexander (son of an Earl). But as Monty's Chief of Intelligence, Brigadier 'Bill' Williams, would later remark: 'Nice men don't win wars'.

Monty *had* won the war. But how would he cope with peace?

Some of the millions of German troops who surrendered in the north to Monty's 21 Army Group forces. 'And so the campaign in northwest Europe is finished,' Monty noted in his diary. 'When I review the campaign as a whole I am amazed at the mistakes we made. The organisation for command was always faulty. The supreme Commander (Eisenhower) had no firm ideas as to how to conduct the war, and was "blown about by the wind" all over the place...he was quite useless.

'The point to understand is that if we had run the show properly the war could have been finished by Christmas 1944. The blame for this must rest with the Americans.

'To balance this it is necessary to say one thing, i.e. if the Americans had not come along and lent a hand we would never have won the war at all.'

Recollections of Monty's War

Brigadier Sir Edgar Williams. We knew he'd arrived. I hadn't seen him, but we were told to assemble in a scruffy bit of desert and to our surprise we were given 'air cover', which we thought was pretty remarkable, we didn't feel we were important enough for air cover!

Before he had even arrived that air cover had disappeared, so there was a fair amount of anti-climax in the atmosphere when he did arrive, this little man; he was more comic than anything else, I think, because he was very small, very skinny: a sort of foxy face. . . I think what one most remembered – of course we were rather arrogant in those days – was that his knees were not only very knobbly, they were very white and it was quite clear that he'd never been in the desert. So he had an uphill job, convincing us that he was the new leader.

He had a very unfortunate, rather spinsterly voice, rather high-pitched.

He made a series of assertions, all, to us, rather dubious.

The first one we all welcomed: that is to say we weren't going to retreat, there was going to be no withdrawal.

Then there was to be no 'belly-aching', which he defined for us as, roughly, discussing orders rather than obeying them.

And then he said: "If the enemy attacks in the next week or so, it'll be difficult. If he waits for a fortnight it'll be splendid. . .then after that we shall attack him," and he went on to say that a lot of new tanks and new anti-tank guns were arriving, which we, of course, welcomed. I remember going away with my friends from this curious conference impressed by the dynamism of the man, but at the same time thinking, well, he's still got to deliver and we've had a lot of generals through our hands, and they seem to disappear – will this man last? That was rather the feeling.

One of the things about him was he always said everything several times, so that although the method of delivery was high-pitched, nevertheless the reiteration gave, as it was intended to give, the right emphasis, so that you didn't forget. As you see, I remember roughly what he said even though it's 45 years ago.

He was an astonishingly good listener and gave you his total attention. It was almost vibrant, his attention, and he didn't question anything you said till you'd finished. And then he'd ask an occasional question, not to doubt what you'd said, but to have some emphasis, or some detail, some extra bit that he wanted to be certain about.

The most extraordinary thing about the first Intelligence briefing I had with him was that he wasn't very interested about the enemy's attack – which was what I thought I was going to talk to him about, because that was the first thing we'd got to face up to – he was much more interested in the enemy *defences*. He'd already got the first battle quite clear in his head, which was Alam Halfa; he was much more interested in what became the Battle of Alamein.

Everybody admired the Auk (General Auchinleck) tremendously, but at the same time realised that he'd reached the end of his physical tether. He was exhausted. He'd stopped the rot twice when other nerves had failed. And when Winston came out and we realised that the Auk was for it, we didn't know what we were going to get in the next round.

Now this startling little performer did immediately create this note of confidence, because it exuded from him and he was determined that he should pass it on and fill the audience, as it were, with confidence too. If you were in Intelligence and knew what you thought was going to happen – to have somebody who immediately took the point, compared with the uncertainties that had preceded: there was the feeling that this *wasn't* improvisation, this was *it*, this was the proper way of dealing with the thing, this was professional.

And at Alam Halfa, it was the first time, I think, that we'd ever seen the German armour turn tail. This little man had said what would happen, and it turned out pretty well according to plan.

The result of Alam Halfa was that it strenghtened the belief in his generalship, so that when you came to deal with the big battle, which had to be a frontal attack, the necessary morale had been created, the belief in this particular Commander: 'O.K., this battle's gone sufficiently according to plan to make one believe the next one will go according to plan. . .'

He never showed any sign of anxiety. It was a performance in the sense that if you don't show signs of stress, you are exuding confidence. You've explained what you're going to do and therefore according to plan it will go!

It didn't – but it went sufficiently according to plan for adjustments to be made, because the overall plan was clear. At Alamein, after all, you'd been told it was going to be a dogfight lasting perhaps 12 days, so you didn't expect quick results.

The armour which General Lumsden was commanding was supposed to get out and beyond the enemy lines of defence. Well, it didn't get out to that extent by the time that had been postulated. . . Lumsden was summoned back to Monty's caravan and there was a row. Lumsden came out much shaken and I don't think was ever given complete confidence by the Army Commander again.

They were different breeds. Lumsden was a cavalryman. I think he'd ridden in the Grand National. He was very well groomed, beautifully turned out always.

Whereas Monty had spotted that quite a number of people in the desert weren't very well turned out and he took to wearing clothes looking as old as ours. So there was the perfectly turned out Lumsden who had, I think, a sort of social contempt for Montgomery and Montgomery had an intellectual contempt for him. I think that partly it was 'gents' versus 'players', but it was also the old cavalry approach to infantrymen. The fact is, Monty's early life in Tasmania had left its mark on him so he was, compared with the frightfully well turned-out Englishman, slightly the colonial larrikin.

I think it was the professionalism of the man which impressed throughout the war – he was dealing with a highly professional Army in the Germans and only a professional could have defeated them... I think he was a very arrogant, very vain man. His great strengths were clarity and decisiveness. In a battle, decisiveness is the most important thing, because a decision, wrong or right, is what you need...

He wasn't a nice man – but nice men don't win wars!

General Sir Charles Richardson. Before Monty arrived in the desert, morale at Eighth Army headquarters was low, lower even than amongst the fighting formations — because we knew much more about the bigger picture.

There was very little clarity in the situation. We didn't really know whether we were going to

fight there or whether we were going to withdraw. I was told to produce a plan to withdraw Eighth Army to Khartoum!

We used to meet every evening, five of us, and look at the day's operations and then at the future: what should be done. There was absolutely no clear leadership.

Auchinleck, the Army Commander, was a great personality: a big man, a man of absolute integrity, of courage, of everything else; but not a great professional. He hadn't really got his ideas sorted out on how he was going to cope with this situation.

Monty's arrival was absolutely electrifying. I'd never served under him. I'd hardly ever seen him except briefly after Dunkirk for a quarter of an hour, when he came to see us, but I didn't really know him.

We were ordered to assemble in this bit of sand, the whole of the Army Headquarters, which wasn't very large, and this figure appeared out of the car in a rather formal khaki with his white knees showing.

Well, the people who'd been in the desert a long time, who'd done 'the Benghazi Handicap' — up to Benghazi and back again — took some pride in their sunburnt appearance and their informal dress. And here was this man in a stiff hat and white knees, and I thought to myself, well, how is he going to fit into this gang of people . . .

So here was this man with the white knees. He arrived, and he told us exactly what we wanted to hear: "No retreat, no retreat — none whatever, none!" And "you'll fight here; if you don't stay alive, you'll stay here dead" — that sort of thing.

At the end of it all, it was so dramatic and unlike the more pompous, senior view of a great general, that one felt a little bit of scepticism: was this just a front or was it really going to happen?

He waved a paper to us and said: "This is what the Prime Minister gave me. My mandate — knock Rommel for six out of Africa", and so on.

It was such a change from what had gone on before. Auchinleck didn't really put himself across at all, even to his own staff — whereas here was this man with this astonishing confidence, promising this change in our affairs, in a high-pitched voice, with constant repetition: and those brilliant blue sparkling eyes.

The impact was clarity, clarity about what he wanted to do.

The first thing that struck me, was this business of going to see his commanders, *all* his commanders, right down to unit commanders and to talk to the soldiers. We called it 'The Circus'; he used to set off at about 7 o'clock in the morning, in that old Humber car — which was very unsuitable for driving across the desert — with glossy magazines and cigarettes in the back, and then he'd assemble the soldiers, on a programme, of course, and wouldn't come back until 7 o'clock in the evening, having seen 20 or so units. 'Bingeing them up' he used to call it — and this again was totally different to Auchinleck.

At his headquarters, his style was absolutely personal as well as professional. He would stay in his map lorry, and spend a lot of time actually looking at the map, which was marked up, of course, with the enemy and our troops; and he would personally make his plan.

This was the thing he always insisted upon: that the big plan, the outline plan, must be made by the Commander who's going to be responsible for carrying it out, contrary to the American practice.

And then, having discussed it with his Chief of Staff to see if he had any points to make, he would go and see his Corps Commanders who were going to carry it out — go into their map lorries and sit down, just the two of them, no staff, going through it all on the map. I can visualise his fingers now, sort of going over the map, those rather bony, long fingers. He'd listen to the Corps Commander and to his views on whether something was difficult, and then they would agree absolutely on it. That was then the plan, and unless the situation changed completely, there was no amendment to that plan.

It didn't matter a damn to Monty whether you were a regular soldier, a Territorial, or a conscript; whether you were old or young, whatever your background was — nothing like that mattered at all. He had a very keen eye for selecting people and once he selected someone, he gave him his complete confidence.

When a divisional commander failed, he often used to invite him to breakfast. He liked to get this over first thing in the day, get it right behind him — he had this extraordinary ability to put situations behind him, once he'd dealt with them. So they were invited to breakfast and he would discuss it with them in a perfectly gentlemanly, courteous way — not so much that they'd failed the Army Commander, Monty himself, but because the soldiers wouldn't believe in them any longer, and then he would tell them that they had to go.

Monty got a great reputation for ruthlessness, but as far as we were concerned in our little, very junior group, when he first arrived and some of our senior commanders were changed, we reckoned that he'd made the right decisions.

He was very conscious of casualties. The first feature of his attitude was that the wounded must be looked after extremely well — we must have a first-class Army Medical Corps, and he took a great interest in that. Secondly, that the battlefield must be cleared up properly afterwards, and that the reinforcements coming in must be inducted properly into their units.

He had a very shrewd idea of what casualties would result from various battles, so that the hospitals could be properly organised. I remember several weeks before Alamein I had to make an estimate of casualties. I'd never studied this. It was one of the things we didn't study, so I went to Freddie and said: "I can't give a figure for this. I've nothing to base it on." "Nor have I, I'll go and ask the Army Commander," Freddie answered — and he came back and

said 13,000: which was almost precisely what the casualties were. Monty had already told us the battle would last for nine or ten days — extraordinary professionalism.

Field-Marshal Lord Harding. Monty's impact on the troops of the Eighth Army — oh it was terrific.

At the time when he took over the Eighth Army, in my view, morale in individual units was all right, but the Army itself was rather at sixes and sevens. They'd had a punishing retreat, formations had been broken up, and brigades had been moved here and there.

Morale was low in the army as a whole. And Monty, by the way he got round and saw them, by the way he addressed people and by his whole style of command restored confidence and morale. There's no doubt about that.

It wasn't a publicity gimmick. The odd bits of publicity, like wearing two badges in his beret and that sort of thing were all part of his technique or style, his style of *command*.

Before the battle of Alamein he went round to divisions in turn and talked to all the officers of the division and told us what was required of us and why, what was the plan of the battle . . . It was remarkable, the skill with which he described his plans in the simplest terms. One of Monty's greatest attributes in my opinion was the ability to reduce a military problem to its simplest proportions. At his briefing of the troops it was very clear, it inspired confidence and it

raised morale.

I was wounded in January 1943, just south of Tripoli. He responded immediately. He was marvellous to me, he really was, and I shall always remember with pride and affection the way he interested himself in my life and my career. Because the doctors had told him, he knew perfectly well the doctors thought I had no future at all, that I was out for the rest of the war. Fortunately they proved to be wrong, but that was the medical opinion at the time, and Monty — he was the best friend I could have had in those circumstances. He wrote to me, and, when he came back to Cairo to plan the invasion of Sicily, I got a message to say that he was coming up to the hospital and would like to see me. I thought he would come and just pass the time of day, sit down and have a talk to me for about five minutes or so, because I knew he was terrifically busy.

But not a bit. He came, pulled up a chair beside my bed, sent his ADC away and spent, oh I don't know, an hour on me, telling me about all that had happened since I was knocked out, and particularly about the activities of my division. That I most deeply appreciated. I shall always remember it.

The following year I went out to Italy, to serve under General Alexander.

I don't think you can compare the two. They were quite different. I had a high regard for Alexander, and a tremendous admiration for him as a man and as a commander, but his style of command was quite different from Monty's.

Perhaps the best way to illustrate this is that Monty was male, essentially. Alexander was more female in the way that he operated — his instinct, his battle experience.

Monty was clear, definite, concise and aggressive, if you like: not abrasive but aggressive. Alex thought that people would do what was required of them without being bullied or dragooned: and that's the difference between them. Alex's great achievement in my opinion was that he held together what was entirely a conglomerate army — the group of armies in the Italian campaign — and kept them facing the same way. Monty took a much tighter control of his commanders than Alex ever did. Alex didn't like to do that really, wasn't prepared to do so. Greatly as I admired Alexander and Slim, if I had to go to war again, I would sooner go under a plan prepared and conducted by Monty than by anybody else who lived through either war.

I would put Monty in company with Nelson and Wellington — Nelson in particular, because under Monty you knew exactly what was required of you, and Nelson was exactly the same with his captains. One of Nelson's captains said, when Nelson took command: it was good to have freedom of action and choice, but to know precisely how far you could go — and I would say the same applied to Monty.

Lt-Colonel Christopher Dawnay. I first met him after he'd taken command of 3rd Division. I was a reservist who had been called up in July (1939), and he came round and inspected the battalion. He spoke personally to every officer. He stood in front of you with those blue, piercing eyes concentrated upon you, and you felt that his only interest for those two or three minutes was yourself. I'd never met a general like that before!

In France, in the winter 1939/40, I was sent up as a replacement for his Intelligence officer whom he had sacked.

He had worked out in his own mind exactly which way the planned campaign was likely to go. He worked out these training exercises whereby we got alerted about midday to move at dusk that night. We would move up to 100 miles south-west across France, seize a river line during the night, be attacked by a phoney enemy the next day, withdraw to a river line in the rear the next night. . .

After each exercise he had his usual tremendous conference at which he told you everything that had gone wrong.

He'd got a brilliant analytical mind, he just analysed exactly how the thing had worked out and why it had gone wrong. We did that once every three weeks and, of course, it was the exact operation we had to do from the time we seized the line of the river Dyle, in front of Louvain, until we got out at Dunkirk.

It was a very small dining Mess. There were about 8 people in it, starting with his Chief of Staff, who was a full Colonel, down to the ADC and myself. He would love to provoke an argument, and would throw out some very contentious statement and invite everybody to criticise it. It might be a military matter, it might be civilian, it might be anything – you had to be very much on the ball. If you made a silly remark, he rounded on you and said, 'That's idiotic, come on, think again, use your brain,' and you did, you became quite lively in argument. . .

He always went to bed at half past nine, war, peace or anything. He never drank, he never smoked, but he didn't mind if you drank. He didn't like cigarettes in his presence if he could help it, and very few of us actually ever did smoke.

He could be ruthless and sack people – even his own people.

I remember only too well, during the attack on Caen, he had a general, Charles Bullen-Smith, who'd been with him at Dunkirk as a Major, whom he'd promoted to command his Battalion, the KOSB, and then later to command the Lowland Division. He was a very brave and intelligent officer and one who had a very good training record. He'd

trained both his battalion and his brigade and his division extremely well. Monty then appointed him to command the Highland Division.

Well, Charles was a Lowland Scot and the Highland Division had been fighting since Alamein, right across North Africa, whereas Charles had last seen action at Dunkirk. And when they went into battle at Caen, the Highland Division didn't fight for him, didn't do very well, and Monty told me to get hold of Charles and bring him up to his HQ not far from the beaches where we'd landed. I did that, and Charles went in and saw Monty.

Monty said: 'I'm awfully sorry, Charles, you must go, the men won't fight for you. You'll go home now. Kit will arrange it all, you will not go back to the Division, and I'm appointing somebody else to take command.'

Charles came out with tears pouring down his face. It was a terrible moment for him and of course it broke him for all time. Monty himself was deeply moved by it, but he said, 'If I don't remove you, Charles, men will be killed unnecessarily. You must go.' That was all.

As regards his vanity, in the early stages he once made a great speech saying there were three important things about command. Commanding an Army, you must make sure your men were well trained. Secondly you must make sure your men were well equipped. Thirdly you must be a leader whom they would have trust in.

However it was quite clear that, having put on that mantle, he could never take it off again. After the war he became extremely vain – but it was that mantle which he had put on for the war, and which was of great value during that period.

<u>*Sir Robert Birley's 1946 portrait of Monty, Commander-in-Chief of the British occupation troops in Germany.*</u> Though depicted as a victorious Field-Marshal at the height of his powers, Monty had been badly injured in a plane crash and was exhausted both by the years of campaigning in the field and his post-war responsibilities. One of his Liaison Officers, visiting him at this time, recorded in his diary: 'He looked older and greyer – like some tired old vulture. . . He neither likes nor understands the problems (of government) but has to shoulder the responsibility. . . I felt Monty had not all the drive and enthusiasm that he had when I first met him (early in 1944).'

Monty in Whitehall. Churchill's original intention was that Field-Marshal Alexander should succeed Brooke as head of the British Army (CIGS) in 1946. Alexander was, however, appointed Governor-General of Canada. This left only Monty, already deeply unpopular with politicians – who resented his popularity – and senior staff officers in the War Office – who feared his new broom. 'He will be CIGS I am afraid,' the Vice-CIGS was heard to say, 'and retire a tired, worn-out and disillusioned old man.'

Although the prophecy was not fulfilled, Monty's two years as CIGS were the least happy of his life, as he fought a lonely battle with the Labour government and fellow Chiefs of Staff he despised; Air Marshal Tedder and Admiral (John) Cunningham.

Chairman of Commanders-in-Chief Committee, Western Union, 1949. 'My new job will be a monumental and herculean task: to weld the forces of the West into an effective fighting machine,' Monty wrote to the King. 'It will not be easy: in fact it will be extremely difficult.'

Given a 17th-century chateau at Courances, near Fontainebleau, as his private residence, Monty was treated handsomely by the French government, but was balked at every turn by his French subordinate, General de Lattre de Tassigny. De Lattre refused to take orders from Monty, inciting Monty to resolve 'never to entertain de Lattre in his house except in the strict course of duty': a prohibition deeply insulting to the Gallic *bon viveur*.

'The Western Union Defence set-up is a complete façade,' Monty told the American Ambassador in London in 1950, 'and as things stand at present the West is indefensible.' Finally, alarmed by the communist threat in Korea, the Americans decided to join the military alliance in West Europe, renamed NATO, with General Eisenhower as the first Supreme Commander.

Eisenhower set up a new headquarters in Paris, with Monty as his Deputy, and it was there Eisenhower himself painted this portrait of Monty in oils, in 1951, before he returned to the U.S. to run for President.

Monty remained in Paris as Deputy Supreme Commander to four Americans: Eisenhower, Ridgway, Gruenther and Norstadt. Having helped the fifteen countries of NATO field a credible defence force, Monty retired at the age of 70, saying: 'I do not think Europe will ever be a battlefield again. Any future war will be fought in Africa or Asia.'

He was awarded the *Médaille Militaire* in the Invalides; but his own government, embarrassed by the controversies aroused by his *Memoirs* (published the day after his retirement), refused him any honour or reward for the ten years he had spent creating the European defence shield.

'For a long time I have led a very active life with no time to live in my own house and see my friends. Now I want to read and to think about the future and generally not to be racketed about,' Monty declared on the day he retired to his converted watermill at Isington in Hampshire.

Monty, in retirement, studying the maps in his wartime map-lorry, housed with his personal caravans in a special barn at Isington Mill. 'There won't be the military work, the important military and governmental figures won't go across the screen, as it were,' his army driver declared. 'And I would think that if he doesn't become involved, shall we say, with the normal life of the village and the country, I would think he's going to be very lonely. I can't think that he will ever, shall we say, come down from the heights.'

'He spends a lot of time in the garden, in the house, its nice garden,' Monty's driver-turned-gardener described. 'But as far as what you and I would call a normal home life, it just doesn't exist, insofar as he's quite alone, there's no family. The Field Marshal, as regards family life, is quite alone in that big house of his.'

Monty, posing with infantry soldiers in uniforms past and present. After writing his *Memoirs*, Monty had written several books on leadership, world statesmen and strategy. In 1964 he was commissioned to write a *History of Warfare*, which sold over a million copies – 'far more lucrative than soldiering – but not so enjoyable,' he remarked. Asked what he most valued in life, he declared: 'the affection of the soldiers who fought with me.'

Monty's last trip abroad, in 1967, in his eighthieth year, to the battlefield of Alamein. Typically, Monty refused to take his wartime Chief-of-Staff with him, lest de Guingand 'steal the limelight'. President Nasser arranged what was tantamount to a State Visit. The bodies of some 8,000 British and Commonwealth soldiers had been collected in the cemetery at Alamein: a sight that would haunt Monty to the end of his life.

Monty in old age. 'I keep going and intend to do so,' Monty wrote in 1970 to a friend. 'But I reckon one would become a bit of a nuisance after about 90.'

In fact, following a bout of illness in 1972, he took to his bed at Isington Mill. By the spring of 1973 he could no longer remember the spelling of Alamein, the proud title he had taken as a peer of the realm. 'A terrible end to the life of a once great man,' recorded Field-Marshal Sir Gerald Templer after a visit in 1974.

Monty passed away in the early hours of 24 March 1976, at his home at Isington. On 1 April he was given a State Funeral at St George's Chapel, Windsor, with Freddie de Guingand, five Field Marshals, an Admiral and an Air Marshal as pall-bearers.

'The Military Knights of Windsor in their scarlet coats bore Lord Montgomery's Garter to the Dean, who laid it on the altar, a bugler sounded the last post and reveille, and Lord Montgomery, lifted high by eight guardsmen, left the chapel for the last time.'

Outside, an anonymous wreath read: 'In grateful memory of all you did for England.'

Military Governor of Germany

Defeated at the July General Election in 1945, Churchill had always feared for Monty as a peacetime commander. Patton, the only other Allied general with Monty's battlefield *brio*, soon succumbed to anti-semitism and dementia, forcing Eisenhower to relieve him of his 3rd U.S. Army command.

As Military Governor of northern Germany, including the industrial heartland of the Ruhr, Monty now ruled a defeated Nazi nation, in tandem with General Eisenhower, Marshal Zhukov and the French general Koenig. His punitive views on fraternisation very quickly softened as he recognized the need to restore democracy and the western way of life in his sector. He decided to reopen all schools and universities at the end of the summer, and to encourage free trade unions and political groups. This attitude upset his American allies in Frankfurt, who were still jealous lest he 'steal a march' on them.

Having laid the foundations for post-war German recovery, however, Monty's attention shifted to the international scene. With a popular Labour government committed to the speedy dissolution of Empire, Monty was certain that he would have an important role to play if he became the next head of the British Army, which he did, in June 1946. Field-Marshal Brooke, exhausted by his efforts since 1939, retired to the country to watch birds, leaving Monty to shake up the War Office, as well as his air and naval colleagues of the Chiefs of Staff Committee.

Monty's new broom failed to sweep effectively. Instead of being able to shape a modern post-war army, navy and air force capable of carrying out government strategy, he could not persuade his Service colleagues to take a 'Combined Service' view.

Britain was bankrupt and, beset by international commitments and problems, lurching from crisis to crisis. Mountbatten handed over power in India in six weeks, resulting in 4 million deaths in the sub-continent. In Palestine the government withdrew British forces from the country it had ruled for half a century and abandoned it to Civil War, resulting in four decades of instability in the Middle East.

In Monty's eyes all this was avoidable, the outcome of weakness of will, of lack of forethought, and flabbiness of judgement: the same myopic pragmatism that had characterized Eisenhower's campaign in the war. Vainly, Monty toured the world and attempted to write his *own* defence policy for Britain — even getting the Canadian Prime Minister and American President (Mr Truman) to underwrite his proposals for a secret post-war military alliance. But without the support of the British Prime Minister or his own RAF and Navy counterparts, Monty was howling to the wind. His warnings and exhortations went

In the wake of Allied victory, Monty was showered with Freedoms across Europe. Here he acknowledges the cheers of the people Liège.

unheeded until, in the wake of the Russian closure of access to Berlin in 1948, the European nations became frightened by the spectre of a war with Russia

For two years Monty had called for a new defence alliance in Western Europe. His visits to Washington assured him that, if the European nations demonstrated a real willingness to defend themselves in war, the USA would provide military help and, ultimately, military partnership in Western defence. As the Berlin airlift reached its climax, therefore, Monty was chosen as Europe's new 'Supremo': Chairman of the Commanders-in-Chief of Western Union, comprising Britain, France, Luxembourg, Belgium and Holland. The Western European defence alliance, forerunner of NATO, had been born with Monty as its boss.

As British Military Governor of occupied Germany, Monty was responsible for some 23 million Germans, as well as the task of reviving the industries of the Ruhr. Here he reviews American troops on the Rhine, with Eisenhower's Chief-of-Staff, General Bedell Smith.

Injured in a plane crash and hospitalised with influenza, Monty decided to take his first winter holiday since 1937 in Switzerland, with his ADCs and personal staff officers. 'I am a poor man. I have no money of my own. All my belongings have been destroyed during the war by enemy bombing – every single thing I possess has gone. . . I have no home; even if I had a house I have nothing to put in it. I have nowhere which my stepsons and my own boy can come to, and call "home". I make my temporary war home with friends, but that cannot go on for ever,' Monty appealed to the King – but no offer of a house was given, either by the Government or by the monarchy.

In the end Monty bought a tumble-down mill and converted it into a house with timber given by the Governments of New Zealand and Australia.

Monty's mother Maud. Defying convention, Monty's mother insisted on calling herself Lady Montgomery – behaviour which not even the Queen dared forbid. As her son Bernard became a household name, Maud revelled in the attention she received, giving interviews and broadcasts in Britain and Ireland.

But Monty could never forgive her failure to show love or affection towards him in childhood, and turned against her once he had achieved fame, refusing to let his son visit her in Ireland ('On no account is he to go; my mother is a very old lady and is quite hopeless with children and boys.'). He also refused to let her be present when he was awarded the Freedom of Newport in 1945, and refused to attend her funeral in 1949.

The First Soldier in Europe

The Labour government was delighted to get rid of Monty. He was as much a thorn in its side as he had been to Eisenhower's administration during the war.

Fame had certainly not improved Monty's personality. He had been made a Knight of the Garter and a peer of the realm in 1946, styling himself Viscount Montgomery of Alamein. Almost every city in Europe had awarded him its Freedom. He was Europe's First Soldier, a hero whenever he appeared in public. But he was an increasingly awkward, lonely, unpredictable man in private.

The death of his wife in 1937, and the long years of struggle to achieve high command had left their scars, and in many

Monty, the CIGS, proudly presents the Belt of Honour to his son David, who had passed out top from his Officer Cadet training establishment. In fact Monty's relations with his son were difficult. Ever since Betty's death in 1937, Monty had refused to allow members of his family to 'muscle in' on the upbringing of David, but had almost no time himself to look after his son, who was brought up by his

guardians, a preparatory school headmaster and his wife.

Monty was strangely impressed by the wealthy, given his absolute belief in meritocracy in the army. When David announced he wished to marry Mary Connell, daughter of a Clydeside shipbuilding magnate, Monty's pride knew no bounds. He offered to buy the engagement ring on behalf of his

son, who was abroad – and during a pre-emptive visit persuaded the jewellers to show only rings below a certain value when he brought Mary to see their 'entire' selection the next day!

When David later divorced, Monty was so upset that for a time he cut David, his only son, from his will.

By 1948 Monty's relations with his fellow Air and Navy Chiefs of Staff had deteriorated beyond repair, and the Prime Minister, Mr Attlee, was only too pleased to get rid of Monty, who became the supremo of Western Europe's new military alliance, the Western Union, with its headquarters in Paris. Like a *prima donna*, Monty was loath to be succeeded on stage by anyone who might overshadow his own performance; he therefore advised against the appointment of Sir William Slim, legendary victor of the campaign in Burma, as CIGS. Attlee refused to take Monty's advice, and appointed Slim as Monty's successor: a post Slim held with great distinction.

eyes he was only half-way sane. When his aged mother was brought to Wales to attend his Freedom ceremony in the town of Newport, without his knowledge or consent, he refused to continue the proceedings until she was removed. He did not even attend her funeral in 1949. He dropped his faithful wartime Chief-of-Staff, Freddie de Guingand, without compunction, and he cold-shouldered old acquaintances who stepped near his new 'throne', as if fearful they might steal his limelight or somehow puncture his vastly over-inflated self-regard. His campaign narratives *El Alamein to the Sangro* and *Normandy to the Baltic* were simplistic and self-serving. Worst of all, they allowed no possibility of Monty ever having made an error. A dangerous groundswell of hostility grew among writers, both in Britain and in America, outraged by his conceit and historical over-simplifications. Better than any commander in the Allied armies, Monty knew that battles do *not* go exactly according to plan, that it is the duty of a great commander to inspire his men to *force* the battle to swing his way, despite all the vicissitudes and failures that arise. Yet Monty in retrospect seemed unwilling to admit to any failings, gilding a picture of himself as a military demi-god. As a result he found fewer and fewer people willing to 'play along' with this grotesque self-estimation. He consoled himself with surprising, even extraordinary, 'affairs of the heart' with innocent children who would not threaten his crown. Far from being homosexual, they represented the somewhat pathetic, platonic yearnings of

an increasingly stern, lonely old widower for simple friendship and affection. These were qualities he ruthlessly excised from his daily, almost ritualistic exercise of military power at the great 17th century chateau at Courances, which the French government gave him as a home and office.

Though generous with their chateaux, the French were as jealous as the Americans had been during the war when it came to the matter of command. The French Commander-in-Chief of the Ground Forces refused to take orders from Monty, claiming that he was merely the Chairman of a committee, not a commander. Work on a unified structure of western defence seemed doomed to the traditional French vices of intrigue and parochialism, driving Monty to distraction.

One again, international events came to his aid. As the crisis in Korea deepened, the United States government began to seek urgently a formal unification of its western allies. This unity could only be obtained by American involvement in the main European military defence organisation. By the end of 1950 President Truman had appointed Eisenhower to be the first Supreme Commander of the NATO powers in Europe, and in February 1951 Eisenhower appointed Monty his Deputy Supreme Commander. The erstwhile Military Governors of occupied Germany were back in harness together, with the resurrection of West Germany's once mighty *Wehrmacht* as their most important task.

The Sparks Fly Upwards

Eisenhower's diplomacy and Monty's crusading energy soon created a military organisation that was to bring stability and security to war-torn Europe. In many ways it was the most successful peacetime military coalition ever produced by a group of independent, democratic nations.

Eisenhower soon left to fight the 1952 American Presidential Election, while Monty, now in his late sixties, remained as the indefatigable Inspector-General of NATO's forces, a sworn enemy of complacency and bureaucratic command, who insisted each year on command exercises on a par with those he had mounted before OVERLORD.

To some extent age was mellowing Monty. Increasingly, he accepted America's right to call the military tune. More and more he adopted the stance of peace guru, determined to see hard-won fruits of European security used for the benefit of international peace and prosperity. All his life he had been a teacher, imparting the skills and responsibilities of command. As retirement loomed he began to chart the story of his life as a lesson in leadership, choosing as his provisional title a phrase from the Old Testament, *The Sparks Fly Upward*. It was to be published the day he retired from NATO, in October 1958.

Monty's *Memoirs* (as they were retitled) certainly soon sent military, political and literary sparks flying. His wartime Canadian assistant, Colonel Trumbull Warren, had warned him of the dangers of criticising Eisenhower, the much-loved Pesident of the world's most powerful nation. But Monty refused to bow to pressure, any more than he would agree to 'tone down' passages concerning his NATO allies, the Italians and Belgians, about whose performances in the war he was scathing. Worse still was his portrait of Field-Marshal Sir Claude Auchinleck,

his predecessor at Eighth Army and later revered Commander-in-Chief of the Indian Army. By detailing the 'dog's breakfast' he had found at Alamein in August 1942 and Auchinleck's contingency plans for retreat up the Nile, Monty deliberately humiliated one of the noblest, if most unfortunate, of British commanders. Soon Auchinleck was threatening to sue Monty in open court.

Monty had wanted to tell the unvarnished truth, in his own characteristically simplistic way. He revelled in the controversy, riding rough-shod over the many hurts he inflicted and the end to his friendship with Eisenhower, who never spoke to Monty again. As always, Monty was his own worst enemy, blessed with one of the clearest brains of any commander in military history, yet almost totally lacking in the traditional British virtues of understatement and gentlemanly conduct.

Throughout his life Monty had urged the making of a masterplan: a clear outline of one's situation and intentions. Yet in retirement, having passed the age of 70, Monty now found himself without a masterplan, living on his own in his converted watermill in Hampshire, inspecting a weedless lawn, wielding his secateurs among close-cropped shrubbery, surrounded by his wartime mementoes — photographs of military leaders and royalty, portraits of himself and his ancestors. It was a 'setting to live in' as the columnist Bernard Levin recorded; 'one never felt that he would re-arrange anything. Everything had been where it was and was dusted and put back exactly where it was and always would be'.

Yet beneath the fanatical tidiness of an old soldier, there beat the same indomitably active, energetic, outrageous heart. When he spoke on defence in the House of Lords the chamber would be packed, and when he began to tour the world for *The Sunday Times* as an unofficial emissary of peace, he was received by Kruschev and Mao-Tse-Tung with more welcoming curiosity than a Head of State. In the United States he was condemned as a pro-Communist troublemaker, but he undoubtedly created immense goodwill in China years before America would officially recognize the country's existence.

To the end he retained a soldier's simplicity and realism, abhorring the American war in Vietnam, not because he did not believe in democracy, but because realistically one had to accept that the world divided into spheres of interest of the Great Powers, and because in war one should always fight one's battles on ground of one's own choosing.

Monty continued to write newspaper articles and books — *The Path to Leadership, Three Continents, The History of War* — but his 25th Anniversary trip to Alamein in 1967 was his final voyage abroad. Characteristically he insisted on wearing his Field-Marshal's uniform, though there were at that time no diplomatic relations between Britain and Egypt. "*Colonel* Nasser will understand the wishes of an old soldier," he declared, and Nasser did. However awkward and

conceited, Monty was still the legendary general who had vanquished Rommel in the desert and at D-day; and there were few who, meeting him, did not come away with the impression of having encountered human greatness.

Monty's boast had been that he would live beyond Churchill's 90 years; but in 1973, after a series of minor heart attacks, Monty retired to his bed at Isington Mill. There he abandoned the fight for life and for fame which had given him such relentless energy. On 24 March 1976 he passed away peacefully, at the age of 88. 'Of course I have led a tough life, two great wars 1914–18 and 1939–45, and immense responsibilities in the Second,' Monty had written to an old colleague. 'And the Germans nearly killed me in October 1914. But I got my own back on them later on!'

It was, in retrospect, amazing that Monty's tiny, bantam frame had lasted so long. He was given a State Funeral at St George's Chapel, Windsor, and was buried in the little village churchyard at Binsted, a few miles from his home: the most controversial, difficult, vain but victorious battlefield general of the twentieth century.

If Monty's relations with his fellow Chiefs of Staff in England had been acrimonious, his relations with his French field commander, General de Lattre, were disastrous. More and more Monty came to recognise Eisenhower's greatness as a coalition commander: and was relieved when, at the end of 1950, Eisenhower was appointed first Supreme Commander of NATO in Europe.

After some weeks of uncertainty, Eisenhower appointed Monty his Deputy Supreme Commander, charged with 'forging the weapon' in the NATO alliance. Soon Monty adopted the role of Inspector-General of NATO's forces, ensured West Germany's integration into NATO's defensive shield, and was responsible for NATO's annual command exercises.

Monty in retirement: inspecting a sergeant at the Chelsea Hospital Founders Day parade, 1959, in the full regalia of a Field-Marshal. During his active career Monty had gained the admiration of millions as an outspoken, no-nonsense professional soldier. He had also upset people by his boastful ego and eccentricities – characteristics which did not alter in retirement. Wherever he went he attracted crowds; whatever he said was reported in the Press. His *Memoirs* were a bestseller across the world, but almost resulted in legal action by his fellow Field-Marshal, Sir Claude Auchinleck. Monty remained prickly, vain and arrogant in peace as in war.

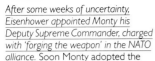

The statue of Monty in Whitehall by Oscar Nemon, overlooking the Cenotaph, and beneath the Ministry of Defence. 'A difficult, lonely and complicated man,' the *Times* obituarist recorded. 'He was, above everything, a soldier. . . He killed the enemy coldly and efficiently; but for the lives of his own soldiers he cared intensely. He was meticulous in preparation, in administration and in execution. He knew his dark trade better than anyone else in his time. He will be mourned. . .as the last of the great battlefield commanders.'

Historians, upset by Monty's boastfulness, were less charitable. The Oxford Professor of Modern History claimed it 'doubtful whether he will be regarded by posterity as one of the great captains of history, or even as one of the truly outstanding figures of the Second World War.'

Recollections of the Later Years

Lady Templer. My husband became Monty's deputy at the War Office. Monty used to ring up every evening, about half past six, after he'd had my husband with him all day and say, without identifying himself: 'Can I speak to General Templer?'

Well, he knew about our household and how many servants we had, which was practically none, so after a bit I thought, well this is too much! So after about a fortnight and this had happened every night I said, when he telephoned: 'What name shall I say?' Ever after that he used to start: 'Good evening, Peggy. . .!'

I think he was a very considerate person, but I think he was single-minded. He was a person who attended to what he was doing and to nothing else. He wanted to speak to Gerald about something, and that was all he had in his mind. I don't think he had any idea that it wasn't polite or anything.

One day he came to see my husband and said to me: 'You look tired.'

I was rather cross and I said, 'Well, I am tired, I've got too much to do.' It was 1948 – we all had too much to do. There weren't any people to help you and we had to stand in queues for the food, and he said: 'Well how do you run your house?'

'Well,' I said, 'I have a daily lady, and a nanny and sometimes a cook.'

'Write down on a piece of paper what they all do and I will organise it for you so that it's all better managed.'

I said 'Very kind,' and thought no more about it.

The next morning the ADC arrived in his car and said 'Where is the piece of paper?'

So I then sat down and wrote it out. Monty went through it properly and said it would be better if the cook did this and the daily lady did that and Nanny did that. And, of course, it *was* better because, you know, anything he put his mind to, he used great clarity of thought and sorted it out – he had that gift which I suppose is why he was a Field-Marshal.

Like all people, he needed family life, and the wives and children of his staff whom he knew well were the nearest thing he could get to it. He'd known my husband for a great many years – it was an ordinary sort of family house, which was what he needed. He'd been very, very fond of his wife and very happy with her; he'd never, never, never have said it, but he was lonely. He used to ring up and say he'd like to come to lunch. He'd seen that my husband was out that day and he would like to have cold ham and rice pudding – it's fixed in my mind because it was always the same: cold ham and rice pudding.

'Well, we don't really much like cold ham and rice pudding, can we have something else?' I'd ask. So he used to come to lunch and have cold ham and rice pudding, and my daughter and I would have something else! He would make us laugh till we cried because he was tremendously funny when he set his mind to it. He could tell you things in a funny way and make them amusing, when he wasn't being a General or a Field-Marshal.

We found him very kind, and a lot of other people I know found him very kind.

For instance, we had a little boy living with us who did lessons with our son Miles. Monty came to tea and he had brought Miles a chocolate bear that he'd bought in Switzerland. He saw the other little boy and said: 'What's that'? – that was the way he spoke. I said, 'Well, that's a little boy who lives here and does lessons with Miles' – so the car was sent back to fetch another chocolate

bear! He was very kind like that.

David, 2nd Viscount Montgomery of Alamein.

I can remember visiting my mother in the cottage hospital very vividly. I can remember being distressed by the fact that she was ill, but assuming she would get better.

My father took command of the Garrison at Portsmouth at this time. He had already warned me that life was going to be different. The first thing that happened in her illness was that she had her leg amputated; my father said: 'You'll have to realise that things won't be the same again'. Facilities were being arranged; there were going to be wheelchairs and such like.

And then she died.

He was shattered. He had an official residence, and the next holidays he and I were alone together. He'd obviously taken enormous trouble to prepare special things for me. . . I was a bit lost, we both were, and I'm not sure whether I was much comfort to him, but he obviously wanted to shower an enormous amount of affection upon me.

I was only 10 at the time, but I don't remember that we ever discussed the matter of my mother's death again.

He liked to put things behind him. I think he wanted to bottle it all up, and that was that. It was a chapter of his life that was over. Therefore he decided to concentrate his affection on the result of his marriage, which was myself: and that in itself presented a problem after a time.

Once he became famous. . .it was amazing. The first time he came back from the desert, it must have been 1943, he stayed at Claridges, where he'd taken a suite with his ADCs. I was invited up from school, and stayed there a couple of nights. Everywhere we went he was mobbed. We went to the theatre and when we got in the box the entire audience stood up and cheered – it was really a very moving experience. In the streets there were crowds and you could hardly move.

And the same thing happened the next year when he came back to take command of 21 Army Group before D-Day. He decided that the whole nation must be mobilised in support of the invasion, and so he started visiting the factories, all the people who were involved in support work. I went on one of these tours. One was overwhelmed by the crowds. He was mobbed everywhere, because he was a tremendously effective communicator.

Once he had achieved great fame, he resented members of his family cashing in on it. He felt his family all wanted to get in on the act. So they were told to shove off. It was as simple as that. And that included his mother!

She was an astonishingly dynamic lady. I can remember, as a small boy, going to Ireland every year. It was an annual ritual and we all assembled in the family home. I wasn't conscious of any tension at all. But when the war started my grandmother decided to dedicate herself to the war effort and she rushed around in Northern Ireland, in the County, doing things. When her son suddenly shot into the pinnacle of fame, this was the greatest thing that happened to her. That was when things started to go wrong.

After I'd graduated from Cambridge I realised I had to make a career, to achieve something of my own, in order to live up to the challenge of being this great man's son. So I lived abroad for a long time. We did drift apart inevitably, partly because of distance and partly

because I was trying to do my own thing, achieve something in my own right. And plainly my father wasn't very happy with the break-up of my first marriage. That disappointed him and caused further difficulties. We weren't really reconciled until much later, when I remarried and decided we must make peace. And we did. In the latter part of his life we became very close again and I was responsible for looking after him. . . I came down to Isington Mill regularly and we became closer and closer, until the very end.

If he hadn't been a general, he'd have been the most fantastic headmaster, principally because of this extraordinary ability to communicate. Another thing he might have done: if the Boy Scouts hadn't been invented by Baden Powell already, something similar to that. He liked young people, and he wanted to communicate ideas. As he got older, the more this became manifest. He felt that young people were more receptive than old people.

Lucien Trueb. I was twelve years old. We were holidaying in Saanen Moeser, my whole family, in 1946. One day my sister came excitedly at lunch time, and said she had heard the great Field-Marshal Montgomery was coming to spend a few days in the snow.

This was a golden opportunity of finally seeing this great man. I skied down the Hornberg and decided there were only two places where he could be: either on the curling rink or on one of those trails

all around the hotel where elderly gentlemen usually take their dignified walks.

Sure enough, he was stomping around in the snow, wearing his characteristic black beret. So I just took my courage into both hands and skied right up to him and said "Bonjour Monsieur", as you do to respectable elderly persons. He turned to me and smiled and said something which I didn't understand . . . Then I quietly slipped off.

Now what I didn't realise at that time was that Monty wasn't just taking a stroll, he was posing for a Press photographer who was at a certain distance with a long lens, and who was taking the whole episode of me coming up to the Field-Marshal and walking next to him and saying hello. This yielded a few cute pictures which were then published in a great many Swiss newspapers, invariably with the caption: Monty and his little Swiss friend.

When this happened I wrote to the Field-Marshal that it was very regrettable, the caption was wrong, but would he please sign one of these photographs for me. Immediately, by return mail, came several pictures taken of himself in Germany, with a most charming letter saying, 'Well, if we are not friends yet, let's become friends. Why don't you come to Berne to the British Embassy, where I'm going to spend my last two days, and then we shall have a chance of becoming friends'.

So I did go to the Embassy. I was ushered into a small parlour and Monty received me as if I were a grown-up person. That's one of the great things about him, he took you seriously. He immediately engaged me in conversation in somewhat broken French; he wanted to know the details of my life, the family, the sports I was doing, my school. So we chatted for maybe 15-20 minutes and then he told me, "Well, my birthday is on November 17th, what about your birthday?" So I told him. "Well, now we're good friends," he said, "so from now on you will write to me on the first of every month and tell me all the progress you're making and how things are coming along." So this very peculiar correspondence started up, lasting 25 years.

The following year he insisted on my spending at least a week in his chalet at Gstaad. At the time my parents didn't talk to me about it, but I found out many years later they had somewhat mixed feelings, because they didn't know what this elderly Field Marshal meant with their son. Monty wrote them a very kind and reassuring letter, telling them that he liked me very much, that I resembled his favourite brother Desmond, who had died at the age I was then — twelve — and that he was getting his brother back . . .

The holiday was certainly one of the great high points of my life, because here was this little schoolboy getting all this tremendous attention from the great British Field-Marshal.

He organised the lives of his ADC's and myself along very strict military patterns. There was an Order of the Day, which was the same every day, an absolute routine. Breakfast was at nine, and after breakfast the ADC's and myself went off to the ski slopes, and we skied there the whole morning and came back for lunch.

Now lunch was a very formal, at least 4 or 5-course affair, and after gorging ourselves with all that delicious food, we went back to the ski slopes, but this time Monty came along. He always worked in the morning. He hardly had any papers with him, but he was thinking, and the afternoon was his half-day off. He came along with us to the Wassengrat chair-lift. Since he had an airplane accident back in '45 he had decided he wouldn't take up skiing again, but he still wanted to enjoy the mountains, so he rode with me up to the top of the Wassengrat and then instead of skiing he half-slid, half walked down the slopes. That way he could see all the beautiful scenery and the people.

Of course he always attracted attention. He was usually wearing just a few old sweaters and the beret was left behind, but he was so obvious, he was the only person on the ski slopes without skis that everybody kept stopping and asking for autographs.

Certainly the affection Monty felt towards me was a mixture of two things: first he loved children; he was magnificent with them; he constantly made miracles happen, which is what children need in their lives; and the second point was his brother Desmond, of whom I was the personification, and whom he thought always miraculously he had gotten back. So the letters he sent me, or many of them, are quite strange, because they could easily be interpreted as love letters.

Now I would attribute this to the fact that he always used a very simple vocabulary. The word 'love' keeps appearing constantly in the letters, but this is a common element he used in correspondence with his friends, with his ADC's, with Lady Churchill — whoever was in his inner circle he just showered with the word 'love'. It was 'love' all over the place, in a Christian sense — I guess he had heard the word a lot in his father's home, (he was a Bishop after all), and so he was using the word in a rather indiscriminate way. But he meant something simple, without any semblance of perversion — he was always expressing himself in a very simple way so that the last corporal would understand his orders. That is why he had only one word for the people he liked — and this was 'love'.

The last time I saw him was in Murren, when I was graduating at the Technical University in Zurich. We went on a walk through the village, Monty with his age-old little cane which he always had in his hand. The military sense of orderliness came through with great vigour still — he was in his early 70's. Monty just couldn't have it that there was dog excrement or empty cigarette packs on the trail. Just like an expert golfer he would catapult these out of the way. Another element which struck me was that he was constantly looking for straight lines everywhere — he'd check the logs in front of people's houses to see whether they were nicely aligned, he commented how nicely the washing was hung up on the lines outside people's houses; he was really the personification of a military man.

Lt-Colonel Sir Denis Hamilton. It was a month before D-Day when I first met Monty. Monty was going round all the Divisions who were going to fight in Normandy. He did it in 3 or 4 Brigades a day. Everything went according to one drill.

He arrived in his Staff car, an open Staff car followed by a jeep. The jeep would stop, a number of electricians would put out loudspeakers, Monty would jump on to the bonnet of the jeep and through a microphone say to all, "Come and gather round me." This was not a military order that any of us knew, and as I'd spent the previous hour drilling my battalion so they'd be absolutely perfect for the arrival of the Commander-in-Chief, they rather looked at each other!

As soon as they were round, he gave a talk of about five minutes. He said: "You know who I am and I want to get to know you". . . He said it was going to be a very tough fight indeed and not to underestimate it, but he would try and limit the loss of life if possible.

He was actually a small man and to the older officers he was always known as 'the little man', rather like Napoleon. But he was taut and tense all the time and when you met him face to face during action he looked at you, didn't take his eyes off you, and many men couldn't take it, the rapid-fire like a machine-gun, the questions. And if you fluffed it, you were out that night. He was absolutely ruthless.

His effect was dynamic in the sense that if he was doing any more formal inspection, going down a line, he wouldn't look at the men's boots or anything. Many generals looked at the boots to see if the men had cleaned and polished them. I don't think Monty was really interested in people's uniform – he never made any comment at all that your men were turned out well or badly, he didn't care about that sort of thing. What he looked at was the bearing of the man's face, and it was a very shaking experience! He looked straight into men's eyes as he went, but this left a memory amongst the men. No other general behaved in this way.

The memory I have of this pre-D-Day inspection was the way he tackled the coming battle. He said, "Some of you will be killed. There'll be as few as possible, but I shall see, and you have my word for it, that you will be reverently buried."

It was a very surprising statement, but it had a great effect on the soldiers, just as Monty's feeling that the second most important man in the Battalion, the fighting battalion, was not the Second-in-Command, but the Padre. He believed very much that the Padre had the morale of the soldiers in his hand.

When I left the army, Monty and I agreed to meet if I went to Fleet Street. When he became CIGS I took him up on this, and within a very short time we were seeing a great deal of each other.

In retirement Monty was very lonely. It was apparent when he got out of the aircraft at Northolt and the guard of honour was there. He was then 70, he'd left his job as Deputy Supreme Commander of SHAPE, he went back to the Mill. There was no private aircraft any more and he didn't know quite what to do. He had really no intention of going into business – a great number of the Service chiefs got directorships in banks or great businesses, which in most cases was to help the man, who often had very little money.

But Monty didn't want that, and therefore had nothing fixed. He hadn't the routine of doing this Board meeting on a Monday and another Board meeting another day, like his contemporaries. I felt he was going to

get himself into trouble in his recklessness in saying things. So I said to him, "Well, your *Memoirs* were a great success, why don't you start travelling the world? There are many places that only you can get into and see the people there. For instance, we're all desperate to know about Moscow today" – so I made all the arrangements and of course he was treated like an emperor arriving. I printed his articles, which were extremely outspoken as you'd expect, but extremely informative too – he'd seen everybody on the political and military side. And whatever nationality you were, or creed, you were couldn't flannel Monty. He was an enormous success for the *Sunday Times*, and it brought him personally a great postbag.

Kruschev's method of tackling Monty was really to make it perfectly clear that Kruschev had all the power and Monty was the retired officer – but within two minutes the tables had been turned and Kruschev was being grilled by Monty, and was making all sorts of promises that they'd look into this and that. They got on the same wavelength and everyone was very surprised when, instead of having one interview with Kruschev, they had several.

The same thing happened in China, with Mao. . .

His last trip abroad was for the 25th Anniversary of Alamein. . . After Monty had laid a wreath at the central cross of the cemetery, which looked so like a typical English churchyard in the desert, we walked round the rows and rows of graves. Suddenly we spotted two graves side by side of brothers, both captains from an Armoured Regiment, who had been killed on successive days. Monty looked at them for a very long time, then quickly turned to me and said, "Let's go. I cannot bear to think of their parents".

He made appropriate farewells, and we left for our little hotel by the sea. We had tea and then walked along the edge of the Mediterranean in the evening sun. He was very subdued.

"I've been thinking about all those dead," he said. "People think

the battle was a walkover because the Eighth Army had been reinforced in September and October (1942).

The more I think back, the more I realise that winning was only made possible by the bravery of the 9th Australian Division in holding the road against counterattacks and slowly pushing forward despite increasing casualties. I do not know of any Allied Division who could have done it. I must go to Australia and gather the 9th Division together so that I can thank them properly".

When we returned to London he started making arrangements, though he was then aged 80. Unfortunately his health was breaking. He had a prostate operation and a heart attack. His doctors said that even if he went by sea, he could not face the huge reception he would be given by the Australian soldiers. After all, he'd spent his early years in Tasmania and always found it easy to get on with the Australians.

Early in 1976 his housekeeper telephoned me to say the Field-Marshal had had a disturbed night and to ask if I could come down to Isington.

I went into the bedroom. I said: "What is troubling you, Field-Marshal?" And he said, "Well, it can't be long now before I go over Jordan" – he never used the words "before I die", never, as I knew – "and I've got to meet all those soldiers that I killed at Alamein, and then in Normandy. . ."

All I could say was: "Field-Marshal, we all knew there had to be victory, that some people would be killed, but you did your utmost to reduce the numbers to as small as possible. You've nothing, nothing to worry about when you get over Jordan – they'll be overjoyed to see you."

K

Kasserine 89, 104
Kesselring, Marshal 59, 60
Kirkman, Brigadier 65
Kitchener, Field Marshal 10
Koenig, General 125
Korea 128
Kruschev 130, 135

L

Lattre de Tassigny, General de 119,
   128, 130
Leese, General Sir Oliver 63, 86
Leigh-Mallory, Air Marshal 36
Levin, Bernard 129
Lewis, Neville 33
Liege 125
Lincolnshire infantry see 'Bantams'
LOW cartoon 87
Lübeck 111
Lumsden, General 64, 65, 68, 85, 86,
   88, 113-114
Lüneburg Surrender 81, 110-112
Luxembourg 105, 106

M

MacArthur, General 95
Malta 60
Mao-Tse-Tung 130, 135
Mareth 87, 88
Marshall, General 95, 106, 108
Medenin 86, 88
Memoirs (Monty's) 120, 122, 129, 135
Messina 89, 91
Meteren 10, 41
Metz 100
Michelmore, Lady see *Montgomery,*
   Winsome
Meuse 105, 107
Mons 10, 29, 41
Montgomerie d'Exmes, Viscomte 98
Montgomery, Betty see *Carver, Betty*
Montgomery, Brian 6, 16, 17, 19, 21, 29,
   37, 40, 41
Montgomery, Colin 19
Montgomery, David (later 2nd
   Viscount Montgomery of Alamein)
   24, 25, 35, 40, 43, 127, 132-133
Montgomery, Desmond 134
Montgomery, Donald 7, 11, 40
Montgomery, Harold 40
Montgomery, Henry (Bishop) 6, 7, 8,
   11, 19, 37, 40, 43, 56, 134
Montgomery, 'Lady' Maud 6, 7, 8, 26,
   34, 40, 41, 42, 43, 126, 133
Montgomery, Winsome (later Lady
   Michelmore) 21, 40, 44
Montrose, Duke of 97
Morshead, Leslie 66
Mountbatten, Earl 125

Mussolini, Benito 25, 86

N

Napoleon, Bonaparte 16, 42, 98, 134
Nasser, President ('Colonel') 123, 130
NATO 119, 120, 126, 128, 129, 131
Nelson, Admiral 6, 88, 89-90, 98, 109,
   116
Nemon, Oscar 131
Nijmegen 102
Ninth Australian Division 61, 63, 64,
   66, 85, 135
Ninth Infantry Brigade 25
Ninth US Army 82, 105, 108, 110, 111
Normandy 64, 70, 75, 76, 98-101, 105,
   134, 135
Normandy to the Baltic 128
Norstadt 120
Norway 64

O

O'Connor, General Richard 23, 38
Oder 110
Omaha Beach 98, 99
Omdurman 57
Operation Market Garden 102
Operation Torch 85
Operation Supercharge 86
OVERLORD 93-100, 129

P

Paris 98, 99, 110
Palestine 19, 20, 37-39, 125
Passchendaele 10, 29
Path to Leadership, The 130
Patton, General George S 51, 74, 77,
   84, 90, 91, 99, 100, 102, 105, 107,
   110, 125
Pearl Harbour 104
Petain, Marshal 48
Poona 23-25
Portsmouth 25-26, 33, 37-38, 132
Poston, John 33, 110, 111
Potsdam Conference 83
Prague 110
Prisk, Major Eddie 76

Q

Quetta (staff college) 23-25

R

Ramsey, Admiral 36
Reggio 91
Remagen Bridge 110
Rhine 102-104, 108-111
Richardson, General Sir Charles
   114-115
Ridgway 120
Roberts, Brigadier 59
Robertson, Field Marshal 13
Rokossovsky, Field Marshal 83
Rommel, General Irwin (later Field

Marshal) 31, 32, 49-88, 96, 98, 99,
   114, 130
Roosevelt, President 58, 88, 94, 95
Royal Academy 75, 76
Royal Air Force 60, 61, 125
Royal Tank Corps 32, 35, 68, 88
Royal Warwickshire Regiment, First
Battalion of 8, 9, 19, 23, 25
Rundstedt, Field-Marshal von 98, 107,
   108
Ruhr 100-103, 105, 106, 108-111

S

Saar 77, 100, 109
St George's Chapel, Windsor 124, 130
St Paul's public school 7, 12, 13, 97
Salerno 91, 92, 93
Salisbury, Frank 82
Sandhurst 8, 12, 40-41, 43
Sangro 93
Second Army 110
Second US Corps 90
Second World War 44-116
Seventh US Army 90, 91
Seventh Armoured Division 66
Sfax 88
Shepherd, David 78-79
Sicily 36, 77, 89-92, 95, 96, 98, 99, 110,
   115
Simonds, General 72
Simpson, General 82, 106
Slim, General Sir William 116, 127
Somme 10, 29
Sousse 87, 88
Sparks Fly Upward, The 129 (see also
   Memoirs)
Stalin, Joseph 44, 88, 110
Stalingrad 53, 60, 63
Stumme, General 64
Sunday Times, The 129, 135

T

Tasmania 6, 7, 29, 114, 135
Taylor, General Maxwell 94
Tedder, Air Marshal 36, 89, 118
Templer, Field Marshal Sir Gerald 18,
   50, 124, 132
Templer, Lady 132
Templer, Miles 132
Tenth Corps 92
Third (Iron) Division 39, 44-48
Third US Army 99, 100, 105, 107
Thirtieth Corps 30
Thoma, General von 85, 87
Three Continents 130
Tobruk 49, 53, 61, 63
Tripoli 31, 49, 86, 87, 88, 115
Trueb, Lucien 134-135
Truman, President 125, 128
Tunis 88

Few Britons have imprinted themselves on the history of their time as Field-Marshal Montgomery – 'Monty' to his troops and to the world. Certainly no British commander is liable ever again to command two million Allied troops in battle – or count such a string of historic battles to his name.

This book has its roots in the idea for a television documentary, to be broadcast on the centenary of Monty's birth in November 1987. I am deeply grateful to Bill Cotton, the Head of BBC television, to Will Wyatt, Head of Features, and to the Producer of the 'Monty' programme itself, Jeremy Bennett. In an age when historical figures are often the target for lampoon or trivialisation, they encouraged us to tell Monty's human story in film, with a proper regard for truth.

It *is* a strange story. For all his simplicity as a battlefield soldier, Monty was a complex man, predictable and yet unpredictable; cruel and yet often kind; boastful, yet often humble; cautious and yet sometimes reckless. Working on the BBC film with Jeremy Bennett I have been privileged to visit, for the first time, the human and military battlefields associated with Monty's

extraordinary life, and was spurred to compress my knowledge of the man (gained during the ten years of writing his Official Life) into a concise narrative, accessible even to those with scant interest in military matters. This challenge has been immensely rewarding, and I have learned much from the Producer, Jeremy Bennett, and his staff that is reflected in this short, but hopefully revealing record of Monty's career, in pictures and words. I am particularly grateful to the BBC for allowing me to use transcripts of new interviews conducted for the programme, only a portion of which could be used in the 75-minute documentary, as also to the interviewees who so generously gave their time to 'remember Monty' in the 100th year since his birth.

My thanks also to the Imperial War Museum, now the repository of Monty's vast collection of Private Papers – as well as photographs, archive film, Monty's wartime caravans, his Grant tank and the world's finest collection of paintings relating to the two World Wars. To the Director, Dr Alan Borg, the Keeper of Photographs, Jane Carmichael, and the Keeper of Documents, Roderick Suddaby, I am indebted – as I am to my father, Sir Denis Hamilton, who, since his days as Editor of the *Sunday Times*, has amassed a unique collection of photographs in colour and black-and-white, as well as documents concerning Monty's life. His help and encouragement, since the project was first suggested two years ago, has been a cornerstone of the undertaking.

Mark Booth of Lennard Publishing seized the opportunity of producing this illustrated book with both hands, despite the daunting publishing schedule. Together with his colleague Roderick Brown, picture researcher Anne-Marie Ehrlich and designer Barry Lowenhoff of Pocknell & Co, they have encouraged me to adopt a multi-faceted approach to the task of pictorial biography and have enabled me, for the first time, to use extensive colour. For all his

eccentricities and inflated ego, Monty was a great soldier and a dedicated servant of democracy as we know it in the West. This volume, published on his centenary, is a collective, honest tribute to Britain's last great captain of war: vain, prickly, magnetic; an inspiration to his armies in his professionalism and concern with casualties; a man who will always be remembered for his first great victory as an Army Commander: a battle which turned the tide of war and restored the confidence of millions in the free world, as in occupied countries, that Nazi Germany would be defeated.

Picture credits:
My grateful thanks to David, 2nd Viscount Montgomery of Alamein, for permission to quote copyright material, as to Christopher Sinclair-Stevenson of Hamish Hamilton and Gladys Carr of McGraw Hill Book Company, publishers of my official life of Field-Marshal Montgomery in three volumes: 'Monty: The Making of a General 1887-1942', 'Monty: Master of the Battlefield 1942-1944', and 'Monty: the Field-Marshal 1944-1976'.
Special thanks also to Paddy (F.S.) Hicks of the Press Association, to Lee Casey of Australian A.P., to Joan Crockford for secretarial help and to Winifred Marshall, my unfailing typist.

Pictures are by courtesy of the following:
Viscount Montgomery of Alamein p29 above left, p33 (painting by Neville Lewis), p75 (painting by James Gunn), p76 (painting by James Gunn), p119 below (painting by Dwight D Eisenhower), p132 right
Tasmanian Museum and Art Gallery p29 above right (painting by Capt Haughton Forrest)
Sir Denis Hamilton p6 left, p7, p9 above and below, p11, p16 above left, p17 above, p20-21, p23, p24, p29 middle (painting by Betty Montgomery), p96, p126 above and below right, p127 below, p130, p131 above left, p134 front jacket
Betty Macdonald p16 above right and below, p41

Robert Hardy Associates, Rainbird and Musée des guerres mondiales p29 below (painting by N S Lytton)

The Imperial War Museum p12, p14, p30 above (painting by Norman Wilkinson), p30 below (painting by Berry), p32 below (painting by Alex Ingram), p34, p35, p36 above & below, p46-47, p49, p50-51, p53, p55, p58, p59, p62, p63, p64-65, p66, p66-67, p68, p70 above and below (painting by Freedman), p71 above and below, p72 above and below, p73 above, p77 (painting by James Gunn), p78-79 (painting by David Shepherd), p79 above & below, p80, p83, p84, p85, p86 above & below, p86,-87, p87 above and below, p88, p89, p90-91, p92 left and right, p93, p94-95, p97 above and below, p99 above and below, p100, p100-101, p102, p103, p104, p106, p107, p108, p109, p111, p111 top and bottom, p112, p117 (painting by Sir Oswald Birley), p125

The Commandant, Staff College, Camberley p31 (painting by Terence Cuneo)

Topham Picture Library p32 above

Popperfoto p35, p118, p119 above, p120 below, p127 above right, p131 above right

Glasgow Gallery of Art p69 (painting by Augustus John)

New Media Productions p73 below, p74

From the painting by Terence Cuneo p81

National Portrait Gallery p82 (painting by Frank O Salisbury)

Life Magazine (Colorific) p120 above, p121 above & below (photos by Mark Kauffman)

Don McCullin/ Magnum p122 (photo by Don McCullin)

Press Association p123, p124 below

The Sunday Times p124 above

State Library of Tasmania p6 right

Colonel Brian Montgomery p17 below

Lady Michelmore p40 left

Jeremy Bennett p40 right, p113, p116, p132 left, p133

Colonel and Mrs John Carver p21, p22, p23, p25, p42, p43

US Army Military History Institute p87 middle

Camera Press London p126 below left (Portrait study by Karsh of Ottawa)

Colonel Richard Carver p26-27, p37 above and below, p38-39

Lt-Colonel C.P. Dawnay p96 left

Monty's unpublished résumé of the Second World War and its leaders, written in the 1960s.

1939/45 War

The 1914/18 war came later to be called a "world war" because contingents from many parts of the British Empire served in Europe, and because the U.S.A. joined the Entente Powers in 1917. But in reality, since the role of seapower was mostly passive, this was less of a world war than some previous conflicts.

The only way for the Allies to win the 1914/18 war was to defeat Germany decisively on one of her main fronts. The Russians were unlikely to achieve this, therefore the Allies had to seek to win on the western front. The French, naturally, accepted this as the main task, and viewed all other ideas with grave suspicion.

— " —

There can be no such thoughts about the war brought on by Hitler in 1939. That war roamed all over the world - it started slowly in them flared up swiftly in 1940; and finally raged over almost all the world and becoming immensely complicated.

National leadership was highly important — all depended on it. Hitler made the most mistakes, finally finding himself fighting the British Empire, Russia, and America — and could not hope to win.

Stalin, a great leader. Only he got the results he sought, and that because his military decisions were taken against the background of a definite political policy — Russian domination in Europe, and the stamp of communism as far to the west as possible.

Roosevelt was never clear about what he was fighting for. He tried to woo Stalin, but the latter won the peace for Russia at the Teheran conference, and Yalta was his greatest victory; he had no difficulty in fooling Roosevelt. When the three leaders met at Yalta they persuaded themselves that Stalin was a gentleman, and agreed to the partition of Germany. They didn't understand that Stalin was ruthless, and no kind of gentleman.

Churchill, a great leader of the British people in a crisis. He had the quality of vision — a quality which entitles him to a foremost place among strategists. By early 1944 he was exhausted, and his power of decision was spent. That was our main problem, together with declining manpower resources,

began to break up divisions in Normandy, believing that a lesser number of strong divisions was better than a larger number of weak ones.

The "captaincy", or leadership in the higher sense, of the armed forces in the various theatres, varied directly with the political control of the generalship.

On the Russian front, the generals did what they were told by Stalin — who dictated the strategy, and very well too.

On the British theatres, Churchill and the Chiefs of Staff were in firm control of the generals. This worked out well, except for the disastrous expedition to Greece in 1941. Churchill was not a good picker (Percival in Singapore, Auchinleck who should have been "left in India where he was an expert).

For the American armed forces, the generals and admirals were in firm control. They considered that all military action must be based entirely on military factors, and political policy would be considered when the war ended; hence the appalling chaos in the world today.

Of the Russians, Zunhov was by far the best.

Of Americans, the only "Great Captain" was MacArthur.

The generalship on the Western front in Europe, and in the Mediterranean theatre, cannot be evaluated without examining Eisenhower's understanding of war.

In the Pacific theatre MacArthur and Nimitz had no inconvenient Allies to suggest alternatives!

Alliances ride the waves of war uneasily, as Eisenhower found! His trouble was not only a lack of knowledge of war; he also didn't like to give orders to his generals; he was a "persuader", who desperately wanted to be liked. He was completely in the hands of his staff. Wavell said of Lee that he was "too much of a gentleman for the ungentlemanly business of war." Maybe that could be said of Ike. Lee didn't like to give firm orders to unwilling subordinates; at Gettysburg the army of the South had no C-in-C. After Normandy the Western Allies had no C-in-C, only a Chairman of a committee — Ike.

ITALY

Returned to England
31 Dec 1943

Sangro
28 Nov

R O M E

Foggia
27 Sep

Cerignola

Bari
13 Sep

Brindisi
11 Sep

Taranto
9 Sep

Salerno

Messina
16 Aug

Reggio

SICILY

Catania 5 Aug

Augusta 12 July
Syracuse 11 July

Invasion of Sicily
July 10, 1943

End of Enemy resistance in
N. Africa, May 12, 1943.

TUNIS

Valetta
3 July

Sousse
12 Apr

TUNISIA

Sfax 10 Apr

Mareth 20 Mar

Medenin 6 Mar

Tripoli
23rd Jan
(16 May to 3 July)
Headquarters while preparing
for invasion of Sicily after
end of N. Africa campaign.

LIBYA

Buerat
14 Jan 43

Sirte
25 Dec